T0149178

From Auschwitz to Zabar's

A TRUE TALE OF TERROR AND CELEBRATION

RENÉE FELLER

WITH RENÉE JACOBS

authorHOUSE®

AuthorHouse™
1663 Liberty Drive
Bloomington, IN 47403
www.authorhouse.com
Phone: 1 (800) 839-8640

Published by AuthorHouse 10/11/2016

ISBN: 978-1-5246-4186-3 (sc)
ISBN: 978-1-5246-4184-9 (hc)
ISBN: 978-1-5246-4185-6 (e)

Library of Congress Control Number: 2016916017

Print information available on the last page.

*Any people depicted in stock imagery provided by Thinkstock are models,
and such images are being used for illustrative purposes only.
Certain stock imagery* © *Thinkstock.*

This book is printed on acid-free paper.

Table of Contents

Dedicated to my parents,
Lewis and Bertha Szobel,
and my brother, Ernő

"A Woman of Valor, who can find?"

Ruth, Proverbs 31

"We travel, some of us forever, to seek other states, other lives, other souls."

Anais Nin

"The privilege of a lifetime is being who you are."

Joseph Campbell

Introduction

What a woman! Wherever she goes, she draws others to her. Like the Pied Piper, she attracts people of all ages. Something about her positive energy, her sincere interest in getting to know each person whom she meets, her modesty and gentle yet contagious laugh. But there are many other layers to Renée Szobel Reichold Rosenstock Feller, an octogenarian who has survived a number of intense traumatic experiences and ultimate losses.

A mutual friend, Ann Granbery, became fascinated with Renée Feller who officiated at the Inter-faith marriage of her son and daughter-in-law, then went on to preside over the naming of her two grandchildren. Ann suggested that I record the life of this eighty-five-year-old woman, that hers is a truly remarkable story.

Renée and I met for lunch at a diner in New York City, where she lives alone in an apartment on the Upper West side. I spotted her as she approached the table, and we seemed to instantly recognize one another as though our souls had met before.

She peeled off her knitted hat, coat and scarves. Her sandy blond hair is short and curly. Her eyes twinkle with the adventure of meeting a new person, a characteristic that I was to learn nourishes and sustains her. She speaks with a slight accent, immediately open and friendly, eyes keeping contact as she tells me in a matter-of-fact way about her life.

She begins by stating, "I don't know why anyone would want to interview me, I am not so interesting." But as she lays out the framework of her life's journey, I am quickly inspired and intrigued.

She describes herself as "a survivor and a searcher." She indeed had survived the loss of her mother in childhood, internment in Auschwitz at the age of thirteen, immigration to America at fifteen, marriage to three different men (all of whom have died), parenting under difficult circumstances of three daughters, one with Downs syndrome, and ordination as a rabbi at age seventy.

When she performs Interfaith wedding ceremonies, she often includes poems by Rumi or Thomas Merton about the beauty and importance of marriage. "Lovers don't finally meet somewhere. They're in each other all along," wrote Merton. Or Rumi says, "The minute I heard my first love story, I started looking for you, not knowing how blind I was."

Renée has been in Jungian analysis and in a Jungian therapy group for over forty years and has tried every "New Age" therapy that came along. She trained with Ilana Rubenfeld to learn her revolutionary healing modality combining work with the body, mind and spirit. On her website she proudly describes herself as a Rubenfeld Synergist who had a private practice in her home for many years.

For decades, due to her early childhood traumas, she was unable to let herself feel fully loved, or to show her husbands and children the depths of her affection for them. Now, an octogenarian, through her grit and determination, after endless searching for meaning and identity, she is finally able to own her feelings, kept under wraps so long in order to survive. She has shed many of the internal scars of trauma and is able to assert herself, own her own voice and proudly wear her Jewish identity. She hasn't just survived, she has thrived.

Here is the story of her double layered life—the layer of anxiety and depression she still lives with and fights every day to overcome, and the curious, vibrant woman who travels by bus several times a week for Tai Chi classes, performs Interfaith weddings around the world, and cultivates an always growing international body of friends through her mornings at Zabar's* and zest for life.

Renée Jacobs

---

* Zabar's Deli and Cafe is a landmark Upper West Side destination in New York City.

Early Life in Rachov, Czechoslovakia

I was born into an Orthodox Jewish family in Rachov, a small town in Czechoslovakia near Hungary. From the eleventh century until 1920 the town was part of the kingdom of Hungary and called Rachiv. When I was born in 1930, it again became Rachov and was part of Czechoslovakia. Then, briefly, from 1938 to 1944, we knew it as Raho in the Maramaros district of Hungary. After the war the name changed again, to Rakhiv, when it became part of the Ukrainian Soviet Socialist Republic. At the time of my birth, one-eighth of the population was Jewish. Eleven years later, when we were forced to leave, 1,707 Jews lived in Rachov, part of a total population of 12,455.

My parents' wedding portrait

My father, Lewis Szobel, was from Beregszaz. Tall and handsome, he was working for a newspaper in Budapest when he met my mother, Bertha Zwecher. After their marriage, he moved to Rachov where my mother's family owned two bakeries. He soon became the manager of one while an uncle ran the other.

The newlyweds lived with my maternal grandmother in an old wood-frame house (where my mother had grown up) attached to the bakery on a large plot of land. My maternal grandfather had died long before I was born. the bakery shop was attached to the house while the building with the ovens where the baking actually occurred was farther back. The home was one story, typical of the area and built so low into the ground that in winters, when the snow piled up, we had to shovel several feet of snow to get out of the door.

My mother's sister and her family lived next door in a smaller house. We had a large garden towards the back of the property, where a small house sat that was rented to strangers. It was a beautiful garden and I loved to spend time there. There were walnut trees, ripe in Spring with giant green spiky balls covering the hidden walnuts inside, and a seemingly endless supply of all kinds of berry bushes, ripe with fruit we picked for immediate eating plus canning to preserve for the winter months. There were snakes too in the garden so that, as a young child, I was frightened to go back too far where the grass was highest.

Grandmother was short and feisty. She worked with my father in the bakery making rolls and breads. We had a family cat that did something to displease her so one day Grandmother picked up the cat by the scruff of its neck and rubbed its nose in the mess to teach it a lesson. Grandmother had been a widow and businesswoman for many years and had learned to speak her mind and entertain no dissent.

Paternal Grand Parents

I used to have a recurring dream that I was a child and went searching for my grandparents who were living in the house connected to the bakery, even though in reality I had never known my maternal grandfather.

We lived a comfortable life, we weren't rich. I didn't know rich or poor but I know I didn't lack for anything. My brother Ernő was born when I was three and a half. Occasionally we traveled by train to Beregzasz to visit my father's parents and relatives.

I fantasized a lot. I imagined watching a movie from my bed. I used to think, "Wouldn't it be amazing if I could see a movie right from my own bed?" It actually became a reality decades later with the advent of television.

Once a rift developed between my mother and her sister, culminating in a confrontation where my mother threw a stone at her sister's home. I never knew the cause of the bad feelings; I am not sure that they even remembered how it started.

I don't remember having a very happy childhood. I have only vague memories of my mother, who was sickly, but I know she was very beautiful as there was a painting of her in our house. She looked elegant and serene, dressed up with furs wrapped around her shoulders.

Mother suffered from a mysterious illness, nobody knew what it was. I always felt I had to watch my step around her. Someone told me she was overly protective of me as a young child, but once my brother was born, he clearly was her favorite. I was jealous of Ernő for all the attention he got, so I vowed to be the child who didn't give my mother any trouble. I wanted to show her I was strong and could take care of myself. Maybe that was the beginning of my survival instinct—to be quiet, follow the rules and expectations—all to maintain some semblance of stability or security and thus win approval.

Father was the one I felt close to. I admired him so much that I wanted to marry him or someone like him when I grew up. He was the main caretaker due to my mother's frailty. He was the person who did the food shopping and kept the home clean.

I inherited my sense of smell from him. We would go to the market where peasants from the mountains would come down once a week to sell their goods. The peasants would entice customers by cutting out a square of watermelon or a piece of apple—samples to taste their produce. But my father had a very strong sense of smell and could tell from a distance if the butter had turned rancid, if the lettuce or other produce had been picked that day or was too old. Father didn't want carrots in the soup if they were not fresh.

In our small town, we didn't have modern medicine so mother was never properly diagnosed and certainly not helped by doctors. She died when I was six.

A pall hung over our house for several months, but shortly after mother's death, my father married my cousin, Rozci, who lived next door. We moved into a new larger house that my parents had been building next to the bakery. (My mother never lived to see it finished).

The new house was nicely furnished although I don't think my stepmother had an artistic sense. A large bookcase dominated the parlor. I remember a set of leather-bound books by Alexander Dumas that I devoured and my father always said, "When you grow up you will get this library."

When my father remarried, he chose one of my aunt's daughters, I thus had a stepmother who was also my first cousin. I imagine the family thought it would be great for him to marry a relative rather than a stranger, or maybe he fell in love with her, I don't know. I didn't like her. In fact, I absolutely hated her. She seemed crude and unpolished, she picked her teeth in public. She wasn't mean to me, she didn't beat me, but she would make derogatory remarks, for instance, that I walked too slow. She was stupid, I thought. I liked her sister better because she was the smarter one, but my stepmother was the pretty one. Maybe that's why my father married her.

Initially we went often to the one synagogue in town. I sat upstairs with the women, the men were on the main floor. After mother died, my father soured on religion. He was against very religious men who prayed on the Sabbath but cheated customers during the week.

I had many friends from school but my favorite was Stefka. Her mother owned the sole bar in town and was known for flirting with the male customers. My stepmother told me not to be friends with Stefka. The more she forbade me to play with her, the more I wanted to see her.

When the troubles began, I could sense things, although no one told me. I was too young. At one point when I was maybe seven or eight, we were taken away from home to another town where they made a big issue about some papers. Since my stepmother grew up in Rachov, she was exempt, but my father, being from another town, was considered an outsider, didn't have the proper papers.

My father, brother and I had to go to a city not too far from Rachov, for several months until the correct papers were ready. We were sleeping on a hay-strewn floor. I have always wanted my own space and wanted to make it pretty, as pretty as possible, even given a bare floor covered in hay. It was my nature way back then, so I tried to make it nice.

We didn't have a bathroom. There were stalls like those in a flea market where one could rent a little space. I don't remember where we ate or where we washed.

Finally we were able to return to Rachov, to our home and stepmother and grandmother. At one point, before we were taken to the concentration camp, my father and many other businessmen went to Budapest. Hungarians had occupied our town. They wanted the Jews, the businessmen, to do slave labor, so our family, among others, decided the men would be safer if they went to Budapest.

We lived a fairly normal life for a while, although we didn't hear from my father. I had my friends, I went to school. But it was a very stressful time and obviously I suffered and still do, almost eighty years later. I just pretended that nothing could touch me. I didn't let myself feel any sadness that my mother had died, I sort of decided that the only way I could survive was to feel nothing. That was the beginning of my coping technique, not to have any feelings.

I had a routine, went to school, and took my studies seriously. My stepmother, working in the kitchen, could see me walking home. She would always comment that I walked so slowly. It was hurtful.

I still have a tendency to do things slowly. I can do things very fast or very slow. I used to dance very fast, jump and twirl around, but returning from school I walked very slowly. Maybe it was some kind of depression, or maybe I didn't want to go home. My stepmother insisted that I be home at a certain time, I always just barely made it.

I spent a lot of my free time reading—heavy Dostoevsky kinds of books. Interestingly, in the last decade or so, I haven't read, but I used to love to spend hours absorbed in a book.

Eventually, the Hungarian or German officers, whoever was in power at the time, wanted to use our house as a command center. In the early 1940s they took over our bedrooms, living room, all the upstairs spaces. We had to move from our big spaces to the basement where there was a second kitchen, a functional place. (My aunt's family was spared because their house was small and a lot of people were already living there). My grandmother, stepmother, brother and I lived in the basement for a while. My father had left us a while ago to stay in Budapest.

In 1944 we celebrated Passover and then we had to leave Rachov. We were supposed to take a certain number of things. Actually we had only our bedding and a few personal items. We were taken, not to the camps right away but to a town, Mateszakla, where there was a ghetto. I remember we set up a space, sleeping outside. Rumors circulated that people were swallowing gemstones, putting diamonds in the toothpaste, thinking they were going to save those valuables.

Time is slippery when you are so young and traumatized. I have no idea how long we were there—weeks, or maybe months.

From the ghetto we (including my grandmother who was eighty-eight-years-old and very frail) were taken to the railroad station. At that point we couldn't take anything with us. I remember that my grandmother got separated from us. Soldiers lifted her up, because she was a little woman. She was lifted up onto a different train. That was my last glimpse of her.

The guards herded us into the trains. (What happened during those days or weeks it took to reach Auschwitz I cannot remember after decades of work on my psyche.) The train stopped and started and was pitch dark. I don't remember what I wore on the train because we were stripped of any personal possessions.

I couldn't find my brother although he was on the same train, but I don't know where. I know I was there but I didn't want to see anything, I didn't want to know anything. I do recall that there was a doctor and his wife aboard and he was ready with a poison. That was the kind of thing I heard but I built this iron armor around me.

When I started working on myself, besides my regular Jungian therapy, I tried every kind of New Age therapy but what happened on that train I cannot remember. How we got any food, where or if there was a bathroom, the smells, anything. It was too horrible so I blocked it totally out of my mind. Other writers have described it in great detail but for me it remains a blank.

Auschwitz

When we were herded from the train, I got off but didn't see anybody I knew, although I searched for my brother. I only remember hearing a voice, a man's voice. He must have been speaking Hungarian because that was the only language I understood. I didn't know Yiddish, although my grandmother spoke to us in Yiddish, but I had always answered in Hungarian. I moved like a robot. I kept hearing this voice, "Tell them you are older." So when they asked me my age I told them, "Eighteen." (I took quite a risk because I was really only thirteen).

The Gestapo barked out, "Left." I remember going to the left. I didn't look where my brother was at that point; I just went left and I never saw him again. I didn't think at that moment, *My goodness, he is going to be killed*, but I later knew he went right to the gas chambers. I wasn't thinking. I didn't know.

When we first arrived at Auschwitz, they made it seem like we were going to... gosh... (a cynical laugh). I remember arriving at the entrance to Auschwitz and seeing that gate with the words across the top ARBEIT MACHT FREI (Work makes you free). Once inside you were led to tables with all kinds of officials registering names. Music was playing. They made it seem like you were going to a spa or something. I guess they didn't want people to panic. We all just went wherever they sent us, like a herd of animals. Again, I didn't want to hear. I just did whatever I was told to do.

Next we went into a very large room where we were instructed to strip. The guards (I don't remember if they were men or women) took all of our clothes and gave us these striped pajamas. They shaved off our hair and I was very uncomfortable with a bald head so I wore my panties on my head. I remember that because I was so uncomfortable.

Everybody had to be physically examined. We were assigned barracks with triple bunk beds. My cousin Rozci (my stepmother) and another cousin, Lenke, were with me so I wasn't totally alone.

Every day we received a piece of bread and soup. I could not eat the soup no matter how starved I was because there were worms in it. So my stepmother and my other cousin shared their bread with me. Somebody in my Jungian group recently described what the soup with the worms was, but I couldn't eat it. I still can see it. It was the most horrible looking thing.

Everybody wore the same rags—striped long "dresses," blue and white or gray and white, like a sack so it would fit all sizes. There were no bras. I guess since I wore my panties on my head, I didn't wear panties. I am assuming, I don't remember. They never gave us a change of clothes or any nightgown.

Each of the many barracks in the area consisted of a very large shell of a building with rows and rows of triple level bunk beds. We were sleeping together in these bunk beds, huddled together like animals. The beds were wide, square-shaped and huge, all crowded with ten to twelve people on each layer. There was no place to stretch out. There was no space.

I was assigned to a top bunk along with Rozci and Lenke, plus others. I had to climb up the bunk frame to get to the top; there were no ladders. From there I could view one of the small windows where the portions of bread they gave us for the day were hanging. That was the only decoration.

I don't know how many of us were there. I only know my stepmother and cousin were with me.

To this day it is very important to me to have privacy. I have trouble sharing a room with anyone. Sharing a bathroom makes me very nervous. I would rather have a closet for a room, alone rather than sharing. I was so uncomfortable having to stand close to so many people, although in the cold weather outside that was the only way to stay warm. But I hated it. So to this day I want space!

Early mornings the guards initiated SAYLAPEL. It must be a German term for lining up every person in the camp. The whole Auschwitz population had to be counted every day. We were awakened at three in the morning and then had to form lines, like a military formation, standing outside for hours while they checked everyone's name. It was very difficult.

We didn't do any work. I was only there three months because they chose the people who were most able to work and sent them to factories. They were always choosing. It was so important, at least for me, to seem healthy and strong.

When I go to a doctor for an exam or anywhere, even now decades later, I am thinking in advance that I must look healthy. I worry, uh oh, the doctor will find something and I will be taken away. It is better now but for decades my blood pressure would shoot way up whenever I had a doctor's appointment because I was so frightened they would find something. They stay with you, those fears.

Look at all the work I did on myself. I was dedicated to doing all that work. I don't know where I would be, what would have happened if I hadn't had all that therapy. I can laugh, I can enjoy people, but still carry all my anxiety.

Before I get up every morning I have to take a Xanax because the anxiety is very strong. I don't want to face the day. I don't know what is going to happen. But I wait. For some reason I don't take the Xanax then, I wait until I am having breakfast.

Sometimes the anxiety goes away and I don't need a pill. I start talking to people and it goes away until about five o'clock in the afternoon. In the morning and late afternoon it comes back and taking that pill is a must, otherwise I couldn't get through the evening.

I had no friends or allies in the camps other than the two relatives. I knew I had to behave, not be seen, whatever I did. I didn't want to draw any attention to myself. Nobody told me that, I knew instinctively that I didn't want to stand out so I kept quiet.

Before we were rounded up, when my birth mother was alive, my brother was the weaker one. It was very important to me to be good so my mother would notice. My brother was her favorite. It often happens that way, doesn't it, that the son is the favored child. Maybe because he was sickly, pale. So I figured if I behaved and didn't give my mother any trouble, I would be favored too. After she died and I had a stepmother who didn't like me, I still tried to be good and almost invisible.

I stayed away from the guards. I knew there were all kinds of terrible things happening to others but I did a good job avoiding trouble. I heard commotion, people screaming, maybe they came in and took people away during the night but I didn't want to know, I did not want to see.

I still do that today to a degree. When something happens to someone on the street, I don't stop and look or try to help. I walk right by. That is how I protect myself.

I hate to be crowded and too close to people. It was so cold there and the only way to keep warm was to huddle together, to be next to another human being. But I would rather be freezing cold than to stand so close to another person.

Every morning, beginning at 3:30 or 4:00, we had to stand in line like soldiers to be counted, standing until every person was accounted for. I remember once just passing out, I was freezing, hungry, and weak, but fortunately that time the Gestapo didn't notice. Others in line helped me up so I could face another day.

Always we feared for our lives because the soldiers looked for the feeble. Once you were too weak to work, you were sent to the gas chambers. We were all terrified. When I was in Auschwitz, I was always afraid. I didn't know what the word anxiety meant or how it felt. I knew I felt fear every moment. It is amazing how I went along, doing whatever was necessary to survive.

After being in Auschwitz for three months, an incident took place that I obviously didn't want to remember. However, one day, when I was about sixty years old, I had a Rolfing treatment. It was very effective because this memory surfaced. It was so traumatic that I couldn't even get up off the table after the session.

The guards had separated me from the group because I had been crying, my eyes were very red. They observed our group and pulled me out because I was sobbing hysterically. The Gestapo officer asked me what was wrong and I said, "I'm scared." He told me to go to the side away from my regular group but I escaped those destined to go to the gas chambers and ran back to the others, the living group where my cousins were. They were so happy to see me as they didn't think I would survive once separated from their line.

This experience displayed a strong survival instinct that I was born with and has served me well. I somehow had the courage to run back to my family and was lucky that the guards didn't stop me.

This memory came to me only as an older adult, during the Rolfing session, because it was so traumatic. What happened on the train I still haven't been able to remember, so it must have been even more traumatic.

It turned out that was the day they selected women to go to another location to do assembly work in a munitions factory. Among others, Rozci, Lenke and I were chosen and taken out of Auschwitz after three months there, to Geistlingin. We worked with older German men from 6:00 AM to 6:00 PM., assembling weaponry. The food wasn't much better, but several times one of the supervisors, an older German person, brought some pears from his garden. He put them in our laps.

When I think of it now, it touches me, this small gesture of humanity. The other experiences I remember didn't touch me as much, but here, a little kindness touched me.

Every day we lined up and walked through town to get to the factory. It was a nice town where normal people lived. I didn't realize there were still normal people who put their bedding in the window to air it out and went through their daily lives as if unspeakable crimes weren't taking place under their noses.

Looking back (I remember as if it were yesterday), horrible things were happening all around me. They were beating prisoners. How could I turn it off? I am amazed at myself, even now, that I just went along with whatever was happening. They were shooting people all around me. I just went along and it's as if it didn't touch me. It's hard for me to believe it, even now. How I could go along, knowing everything, but I just didn't want to know.

Now, in hindsight, it's really amazing. I had to just get through the day, one day, one hour at a time, just survive, so I tuned off all my feelings, all my memories and worries.

I was among my cousins and the youngest person in our barracks. All the people I knew from the camps were somewhat older than I was. I had to live the part of this eighteen-year-old, when I was really only thirteen and fourteen. I didn't really know what it was to be a child because of my traumas way before being sent to Auschwitz and I clearly had no experience being a teenager, but I managed to carry out that charade.

For many, many years I talked to my group and my therapist about this, that I just took it as very matter-of-fact, no big deal. I didn't let it touch me, but when I think of it now as an eighty-five-year-old woman, I suddenly can acknowledge that it was pretty terrific that I was resilient and survived the camps. Everybody I told my story to thought it was amazing, to survive being so young and motherless, but I kept telling myself, *just do what you have to do.*

Now, as I am recalling the past, I can't believe it, I can finally let myself feel some pride. When I told my story years ago to the Shoah Foundation, I was much more matter-of-fact. I didn't think what I am saying now, I didn't feel I should be admired to do all I did. Interesting timing, isn't it?

We stayed in another barracks (not the kind in Auschwitz), from the months of September, 1944 almost to the end of the war. It was a home of some kind. I remember falling once. There was a huge bathroom with a cement floor that was slippery. I fell on my back. I could hear bone against bone, that's how skinny I was, and I have had back trouble ever since.

The food was not much better but at least they gave us potato peels. I must have been hungry all the time, so my fantasy was that if we ever got "home," whatever that was, I would be happy someday just eating my fill of potato peels. Not even a steak, just peels. Peels were like a delicacy then.

I couldn't even imagine that normal life was going on for some people. People who lived with bedding airing out the windows. People who sat down at meals together. We never saw the townspeople but they must have been right there. Every morning we marched past their houses and returned every evening.

When it was getting near the end of the war, we were moved to another camp. As the American allies got closer, the Gestapo kept moving us farther and farther away on some kind of train. Time didn't mean anything. We heard the noise of the bombs and the guns going off in the night. There were hints that something was happening, both prisoners and guards were whispering.

I remember at one train stop we suddenly saw packages started falling from the sky. I don't know who sent them, maybe the Swiss or the Red Cross. Someone was distributing food from the planes although we were still prisoners of the Germans. We were only women as the men had long ago been taken for hard labor.

While we were on the train, I remember lying on the hard floor in such pain because of that fall in the bathroom when I landed on my lower back. No wonder I have always had back problems as an adult.

When finally the train stopped, we knew something different was going to happen. Then the Americans came. It was all so unreal. I wasn't thinking, I wasn't feeling, but I sensed and hoped something good was happening.

Leaving the trains, we saw Americans dishing out soup from these tremendous pots. The first English words I heard were "Go back!" It's funny how I don't remember other things but I knew what it meant because everyone was pushing ahead to get to the food. We were standing in line for it and everyone was shoving, desperate to get something warm and tasty. My stepmother and cousin were with me.

For me it was a very chaotic time. There was no order. I was almost wishing to be back in the concentration camp because at least there was a schedule. You knew what you were supposed to do, you had a routine.

Here you were just let loose. People were breaking into factories, there was total chaos.

It was very upsetting because I wanted to have structure. It was a horrible time, not knowing where to go, what to do. I remember thinking, *Gee, I wish I were back in the camp.* We were kind of lost. I felt very insecure. I missed a sense of order, a plan for the day.

We were liberated near the Sudentenland, in Czechoslovakia, where there were many empty houses that the owners had abandoned. Apparently someone arranged to place us in those houses where groups of former prisoners moved in together. My cousins and I and some strangers lived together in an assigned house. Two of those strangers discovered that they were relatives.

HIAS (the Hebrew Immigrant Aid Society) and the Jewish Federation were involved in locating refugees and placing some of them with sponsors. They gave us packages of food, bedding, clothes and basic supplies.

A few months after we were liberated, a huge feud broke out. My cousins from my mother's side of the family and I had been together in the camps. But it was somehow arranged that I would be sent to Prague with my father's side of the family, my paternal aunts. My mother's family did not come with me.

Two aunts, Agnes and Sara, were with their husbands, another aunt, Regina, was there too. One aunt had been in Auschwitz when I was there but in a different barracks so I never saw her. Her husband had been serving in the Russian army. The other husband was very quiet but he made sexual advances to me. I wasn't molested as I was able to push him away but it frightened me. I never told anyone.

We stayed in an apartment filled with bedbugs. I was sleeping on the kitchen table to avoid the bugs. (There were lots of bedbugs in Auschwitz also, so you couldn't really sleep).

Then there was a feud between my mother's side and my father's side. I was in the middle. I always liked my father's side better because I saw them as more intelligent but the Jewish Federation in the United States was able to find my mother's brother in New York. He had to sign an affidavit that he would sponsor me, which kept me out of the displaced persons camps.

When I came to New York, I stayed with my mother's older brother and his wife, whom I had never met. I don't know how he was so smart to come to the United States before the war. Interestingly, I also had uncles from my father's side, two brothers who also came here earlier. One was a communist, but I wasn't placed with either of them.

I found myself now separated from my mother's side, which created this feud. My aunt, my father's sister, was talking against my stepmother. It's kind of comical in hindsight. I survived the camps and now they were ridiculously bickering over where I should be. I was in the middle and couldn't decide which side I should choose or wanted to be with.

As it turned out, I went to New York with my father's family to live with my uncle who was on my mother's side of the family. I don't remember talking about this with anyone or how it happened. Somehow or other it must have been a Jewish organization who arranged it.

My mother's oldest brother sent papers so I wound up eventually in New York. In order to survive, I had to go wherever they told me but my instinct also guided me. I knew what was good and what was bad for me. My paternal aunt didn't want me to like my stepmother because, according to her, they were all horrible people on that side. The whole thing was nonsensical.

The last I saw of my father was before the war, when he fled to Budapest with the other Jewish businessmen. When I came to this country in 1945, the Jewsih agencies helping refugees could no trace of him. A cousin who was able to stay in Budapest during the war and survived later told me that my father had heard we were taken and had perished as he didn't try to save himself. I was never able to learn how, where, or when he died.

After the war, when I briefly stayed with my father's sister in Prague, she told me that the family didn't know what had happened to him. The only people who knew a little about my father were his cousins, who had never left Budapest and were never taken to any camps. One of those cousins now lives in Florida. She and her parents knew a little about my father, but it is all very unclear.

*Szobel family, my brother and I in front behind
grandmother, Father (tallest one) and his siblings*

My family name was Szobel. In Hungarian the "Z" is silent. Once in America I dropped the Z so it became Sobel. My first name was originally Renée. When the border changed and we were thus residents of Czechoslovakia, my name became Renata but everyone called me Renika, an endearing name. People talk now about dysfunctional families. I certainly came from a dysfunctional family and led a dysfunctional life!

Adapting to America

My aunt Regina came with me to Stockholm, via Frankfort on the first or second transport of refugees out of the camps. We were cabin mates on a ship called the Grigsholm. The other relatives came at different times. Agnes, who was pregnant, and her husband came later on a different boat. Regina lived for a while with Agnes, then moved to Great Neck to be near her son.

At age fifteen, when I left Europe after the war and was traveling to a new country to live with relatives I didn't know, I wasn't thinking or feeling. I was in the camps exactly a year. We went there in April, 1944 and were liberated in April, 1945. For the first months after liberation we lived in total chaos.

In December, 1946, when I came to New York, I didn't yet look like myself. On a starvation diet for a year, we were all skin and bones. We had lost a tremendous amount of weight (my menses had stopped). My hair started to grow back but I never saw myself as attractive.

My mother's brother was in the United States way before the war. I assume the Jewish organization had contacted him. I don't know how this was arranged. I didn't know them in Rochov. I don't know how he even got here as he wasn't a sophisticated man. He was a watchmaker, not very worldly and yet he ended up coming here very early. I am just now thinking to myself it is pretty amazing that he came here. He worked in a building in Times Square. Although the shop is no longer there, I still think of him when I go up and down the subway stairs.

My uncle's wife picked me up where the boat docked. I remember seeing the Statue of Liberty but I was so overwhelmed with all the relocations and dislocations that I had no emotional reaction to Lady Liberty. We took the subway and went up to the Bronx. I didn't know when asked decades ago what I was feeling in those days; it took me more decades to recall those memories. I just knew I had to do what people told me. **It was all about survival.** Thinking or feeling was not in my vocabulary at that time. I just went along.

I moved in with my uncle and his wife, who never had children. They had an apartment with one small room, a kitchen and a tiny hallway. I slept in the hall so anybody who came there had to go past me.

First home in America, with aunt and uncle

I did see a social worker while I was staying with them. I probably told her about my situation, that my aunt and uncle never had any children, their apartment was too small and it was very difficult for me there. So the Jewish Philanthropy found me another place to live after a few months, as it was impossible to stay there.

I remember all the places but the timeline is very blurred. For example, initially I thought I was with my aunt and uncle a short time, but now I realize it must have been for a while because I went to high school and night classes, was babysitting and dating.

The agency then found me a place in Brooklyn with a lady who needed a boarder. Her daughter had left to get married and she was lonely, plus she was compensated by the agency for taking me, so I stayed there for a while. It also wasn't an ideal place for me, so I eventually left there.

The agency social worker then found me a place on the Upper East Side in the 60s, a mansion named Clara D. Hirsh, a way station where young girls from out of town came to stay for brief interludes. It was a supervised place, very secure; you had to sign in and be inside at night by the curfew.

My whole education was so broken up. When I was staying with my aunt and uncle, I went to night school to learn English and to Christopher Columbus High School during the day. It was a walk from where we lived, past the Bronx Zoo.

There were some Jewish students among the mostly white and Christian ones at this high school. I was the first refugee, the first foreign person to attend there, so I was a big hit. I was the only one who didn't wear lipstick. I was different but I made lots of friends. People often told me I looked like Lauren Bacall.

I made friends wherever I went, not like my relatives who stayed with their own, with other Hungarians in their own kind of shtetl, even though they were free in America.

I was doing a lot of dating then, mostly foreign boys I met at night school, as they were more mature than guys my age in high school. It was a problem because young men were walking me home and my aunt and uncle weren't used to this.

In addition to evening school, I got a job through a relative who was originally from my hometown. I worked for a jeweler putting straps on watches. Before that I had a job folding dusting rags in a factory where I sat at a table folding cloths by hand for hours. I met lots of people there, including a woman who introduced me to her son.

When I moved to the Clara D. Hirsh Residence, I was eighteen. During my stay there I met my first husband. At some point I went to Fordham University where they accepted me without a high school diploma because I had life experiences.

All my education is very fragmented because I lived in so many places. I am amazed how many educational institutions I attended without credentials. I was very sociable and went out a lot, meeting all kinds people.

First Marriage

I met my first husband, Kurt Reichold, at Cafe Vienna on Central Park West. It was a place for young people to go and socialize. Every Sunday afternoon Cafe Vienna held dances and there were also tables set up around the dance floor, where single women would sit alone or with girlfriends and hope to be asked to dance. I wasn't thinking of getting married but I wanted a home. That was the main thing. I was tired of going from place to place.

He was eight or nine years older than I was, an intelligent man, who loved music. But being in love wasn't in my mind at all. I was sitting at a table with friends and he approached, inviting me to dance. I didn't wear a hat or gloves but I did have on a scarf. As far as I can remember, and to the present, no matter the weather, I always wear a scarf around my neck.

Kurt was in sales, representing a company that sold or leased concession machines. Later in our marriage he tried other jobs, always the entrepreneur trying new ideas. We only dated a short time. Because he was eight or nine years older, he was eager to get married. He was very interested in me, (it never occurred to me that I could choose as well). He was mature, a decent man from a German-Jewish family.

I didn't realize until much later that he had a disease. He was manic-depressive. Life with him became frightening, because he was a sick man. It was like clockwork, six months up and six months down.

Not every bi-polar person manifests that way but he was regularly up and down. When he was up, he did some wild things. And I really had no place to go. So I was stuck in this relationship for almost ten years.

When I met Kurt, he was very eager to get married and to have a baby, and I was eager to have a stable home and security. I don't know why he was so anxious to have a child but I was too young to have a baby. I hadn't even asked myself, *Do I want to have a child?* I thought about this years and years later. When he said, "You should have a baby," I thought this was what I was supposed to do and I was afraid to disagree with him.

He never hurt me physically but he had a violent temper, especially when he was in a manic phase. He didn't like it when I disagreed with him. He was very forceful, almost like being raped. He wouldn't let us use any birth control and I was very unsophisticated, stupid about many things.

It was a very difficult time because I wasn't ready to be a mother (I was only nineteen but still felt like a child) and, besides that, he had all these problems. He suffered a lot too; it is a horrible disease and at that time all the doctors could offer him was electro-shock treatments. Now they have many medications.

We lived at 195 Claremont Avenue, right near Columbia University and Barnard College, a stone's throw from the Union Theological Seminary. It is still the same today as it was then. The tall brick and stone apartment buildings stand with dignity as ever, my former apartment building has the same front. The sidewalks embrace lovely trees and are filled with a mix of students and families, all ethnicities and races.

It was my first apartment as an American, as an adult. I tried to decorate it and make it attractive. Making my personal space as beautiful as possible has always been important to my soul.

My first daughter, Barbara, was born during this marriage. At first, possibly for a long time, I was afraid to touch her, afraid maybe she would break or get hurt, as if she were some kind of china doll. I had a difficult time nursing her so for months she cried a lot and I cried too, out of fear, frustration and loneliness. When she was laughing and playful, I could enjoy her.

We often went to the neighborhood playgrounds where I met other mothers. Most of the time this was a very pleasant escape from the tension at home, but sometimes Barbara was very aggressive with the other children there and we had to leave.

She was very intelligent but difficult behaviorally. I think she was acting out her anger towards my sadness and the tension in our home. She was always a high energy, intense and challenging child. (In his good moments, Kurt was very proud of her and her accomplishments). She was a top student in school and a very talented pianist. I always made sure she was nicely dressed and I kept the house very clean but I couldn't let myself be loving or affectionate with her, although I do remember kissing her a lot.

Years later, a relative told me that my mother had been the same way with me. She fussed over my physical needs but was not emotional or nurturing towards me. I didn't give her the kind of mothering that every child deserves. I didn't have it to give. I very often now think about that and I feel very guilty. I always feel guilty, guilt is my middle name. Maybe if I had started therapy early on, I would have had more to give.

Kurt had powerful mood swings. When he was up, he would disappear for days or hours. He was entrepreneurial and started many different businesses. When he was depressed or "low," he was quiet, sad, just sitting around all the time and I didn't like that either. His sister lived nearby but none of his family came around much or offered to help with Barbara.

You know, it was so horrible I don't even want to go there. Being in the Holocaust was certainly no picnic but all these things that happened with my first husband, I almost hate to talk about because it was quite horrendous. I was so lonely because I couldn't share my situation with other people, whereas in the camps, you had each other for support. I couldn't tell anybody, I had no one to tell, no place to go. I couldn't say, "I'm going back home."

My relatives who came after the war at different times all had their own lives. My aunt that I came over with moved to Great Neck because her son lived there. Another aunt went to Brooklyn to be with her family. They were busy with their own lives. My stepmother got remarried to a widower with two children. She seemed happy, whatever that means. Her sister (the one I mentioned liking better because she was more positive) got married as well.

None of my family lived nearby or offered to help me. My in-laws did not want to get involved and refused any help. During the marriage and after the divorce they had no relationship with their granddaughter.

When Kurt was high, he didn't go shopping extravagantly but he did insane things. He was arrested once, driving upstate in Salem, New York. They put him into jail. Then he tried to burn the jail down, setting a fire where he got burned, so they put him in Creedmoor Psychiatric Hospital.

During his incarceration some people advised me and then assisted me to go to Mexico to get a divorce. They had known for years how difficult my situation was. Friends found a lawyer who specialized in quick Mexican divorces in a town on the Texas border. A good friend in the next building took care of Barbara overnight. I was gone only for a day, leaving New York married and coming back divorced.

I felt safe while he was in jail, able to make this life-changing move, as he couldn't bother me, but once he was transferred to the hospital, he tried many times to contact me. I couldn't have gone for a divorce while he was around even though I knew almost from the beginning of our marriage that he had a sickness that made it very difficult to live with him.

When he was in a manic phase, he always made money with one entrepreneurial business after another, one day in the vending machine business, the next day on to something else. During those episodes I would squirrel away a little money so when the opportunity came to get the divorce, I had enough funds put away.

Once he was released from Creedmoor Psychiatric Hospital, even though we were divorced, he would call or show up at unexpected times and talk as if we were still married. Barbara and I were often traumatized by his erratic and occasionally threatening behavior. So it was a very difficult marriage, a stressful time, but once again, I survived.

How I developed into a more worldly person amazes me, but I was always very curious. When someone suggested a self-help program, a new therapy he didn't know much about but would I be interested, I said, "Yes." I always say yes to trying something new or going along with others.

I gravitated toward being with a variety of people—more sophisticated New Yorkers. I didn't want to associate just with survivors. I went once to one of their meetings and it didn't do anything for me. I wanted to separate myself from other survivors or fellow Hungarians, while they wanted to stay with only their own kind.

As I became more social, I was always observing people. listening to their conversations, eager to learn about this (for me) relatively new culture. For example, people would talk a lot about food, what they ate, where they dined, and I felt embarrassed. To me coming from Czechoslovakia, it was a *shonda*, something almost sinful.

Beginning during this difficult time I established a pattern that continues to this day. I go every morning to a nearby coffee shop for some quiet time. All the waiters get to know me. For many years I wanted to sit alone, comfortable to just watch the people but not interact. Now I seek out interesting conversations because of my curiosity about people. My need to understand what is happening in the world and to build connections with other cultures has overcome my shyness.

Second Marriage

It was very important to me to be married, to belong with somebody, so I married again quickly. My second husband, Steven Rosenstock, I met while ice skating. (I always found it easy to meet men). He was a very decent man.

Even then, I didn't know what it was to feel or to be in love but I would say this relationship was the closest I came because we had a lot in common. After dating for a few months, we were married in a synagogue in Washington Heights and had a reception there with family and a few friends, mostly Steve's. He was very musical, as were all my husbands. Before we went to an opera, Steven would read the whole libretto and tell me in detail about the storyline.

Steve's friends were very well-educated; they loved classical music and the opera. I learned to dance because Steve was a terrific dancer. I had a friend who only wanted to marry someone very successful, very rich. I'm not like that. It never occurred to me. I never worried what kind of provider he would be, I just enjoyed his company and circle of friends.

I had two children with him. And of course I brought Barbara, who was nine years old at the time, into our household. About a year after we married, my second daughter, Alice, was born with Down Syndrome. I didn't know during the pregnancy or for several months after she was born that Alice would have problems. "I wanted you to enjoy her for a little while," the pediatrician told me months after the birth. (She was a very nice person, a German lady). I took it like every other unfortunate situation, I didn't cry or get panicky. I just carried on.

Barbara, me and Steve

I wanted to have a third child because I had this little girl who was sick, disabled, and I wanted another. A year and a half later, Pamela was born. Throughout the child-rearing years the other two children definitely suffered because I gave most of my attention to Alice.

Having a child like Alice was another very difficult time. The guilt I felt and the challenges of raising her wore me down. Instead of bringing her up like I did her sisters (according to my therapist), I saw myself in her. She was the "weak" child so I did everything for her. I know now that I overdid it. Barbara, the eldest, felt resentment for years. Both girls suffered because they could feel I favored Alice. I did give everything I had to her. She lives in a group home now.

So I went from one difficult situation to another. It is amazing. It's like the book by Rabbi Kushner, *Why Do Bad Things Happen to Good*

People? Even with my therapist, it took a long time to talk about these things.

Steve and I on our honeymoon

At the beginning of my second marriage, we moved to upper Washington Heights, an area called Inwood on St. Nicholas Avenue. We moved into a cooperative. We had a beautiful view of the river, we were so high up on a hill. I didn't appreciate it then.

During those years with Steven, Kurt would often try to contact us, though Barbara was afraid of him and had no interest in seeing him. He had suffered from the smoke inhalation when he set the jail on fire in a manic episode.

Surprisingly, he married again but he was never healthy. He started to have problems with his hip and needed a hip replacement but he was scared to have it. For the rest of his life, he was in a wheel chair. When he was manic, he still would call me, but otherwise I had little to do with him. He died about seven to ten years ago.

I no sooner came home from the hospital after delivering Pamela than I was rushed back. I woke up in the middle of the night in a pool of blood, hemorrhaging badly. An ambulance rushed me to the hospital and I had to have a partial hysterectomy.

Not a secure start for a new baby. Pamela was always a quiet, shy child. By age six she barely spoke to anyone. She suffered from social anxiety and found it hard to form relationships. She was closer to her father than to me although she seemed distant from both of us. She attended public school except for sixth grade.

We thought she might do better in a small, private school so we sent her to a nearby Yeshiva even though our family had little to do with traditional Judaism. She was miserable there so she finished her education at a public school.

Steven was very sensitive and I knew I couldn't scream or show anger directly because he couldn't take it. My third husband, Bob, could take it; we were both very strong. But Steven couldn't stand any arguing; he would have been destroyed.

Basically a quiet person, he had a loyal group of friends from his school days but he was uncomfortable being social around new acquaintances. He could be friendly with those he didn't know and wouldn't see again if he had to, but at home and around most people he was somewhat withdrawn. Most men are happy if you leave them alone but he liked to do fun things with me. I just couldn't express any anger or negative feelings because he couldn't handle it.

He was very active and I liked that. He was a good dancer so I learned how to dance from him. We had a busy social life with his friends and their spouses. I found the men very interesting to talk with as they were all well educated and had many interests. I learned a lot from them. I wasn't so friendly with their wives outside of our couple parties, but I had some friends of my own, mainly the mothers I met at the playground when Barbara was little. I started therapy during this time. I was not easy to deal with. I took out my frustrations on my children.

Steven wasn't that successful so times were hard financially. He graduated from Berkeley College in California but he really didn't use his education. He worked for a real estate company and then decided to go out on his own, managing co-op buildings.

Unfortunately, he got sick just when he started to become very successful. He wasn't a strong person. I guess he accomplished what he set out to do but his health got in the way. He smoked a lot, using that habit to deal with suppressed angry feelings because he avoided any conflict. When I realized he was dying, I knew I would be devastated.

I started to prepare myself to be alone. I am embarrassed to say this but I went out by myself sometimes at night, dancing at Roseland Ballroom or I would just go somewhere for coffee. I even went by myself to Puerto Rico for a few days. I was running, running, running. I was uncomfortable at the time doing all these things but I felt desperate, compelled. This is the way I survived.

Steven's mother was very overpowering. He had a lot of issues with her. He remembered that growing up she had given him a very hard time. Because of her, Steven saw every woman as his mother in a way.

His father died before we were married. My mother-in-law moved to Florida and remarried there so she was out of my way. She didn't come to visit very often although she did fly up to help out when the girls were born. She didn't have a close relationship with Pamela, her granddaughter, and never really had anything to do with Alice.

Pamela and Barbara were always resentful that I was so attached to Alice. Barbara was twelve years older than Pamela and was very sociable so she was less affected by my lack of attention, but Pamela grew up jealous and also embarrassed by Alice, who is very low functioning. Her father favored Pamela and gave her more attention because he felt I was too focused on Alice. Pamela was devastated when her father died, even more so when I remarried. She had a hard time accepting my new husband into our life.

Third Marriage

Steven died after sixteen years of marriage. He was a heavy smoker and died from lung cancer. Very soon after he died, I met Bob Feller, my third husband, a widower. Instead of staying by myself for a while, a much healthier thing to do, I married quickly once again because I really didn't feel strong enough to manage by myself. I was married to him the longest, thirty years. He died of a heart attack; he didn't suffer. It wasn't a bad marriage. I always married good decent men, even Kurt, in the beginning.

Bob and I at my daughter's wedding

Bob was an outgoing person, quite different from Steven. He was an only child. Both of his parents were deceased so it was basically just the two of us. Bob had been married before and had a twenty-year-old daughter when I met him. His daughter, Karen, got married and sometimes didn't call her father for weeks at a time.

I didn't appreciate how smart Bob was because he himself didn't appreciate it so I went along. Instead of building him up, I used to knock him down out of my own insecurities. I have had much guilt about that for many years. Sometimes I just couldn't believe some of the things he would predict and they would come true. I don't know if he was psychic but he was the kind of man who should have been far more successful in his life than he was.

The reason he wasn't, he didn't have enough self-confidence. He would cover up his intelligence. Once in a while he wouldn't cover it up and the things that came out of his mouth were just amazing! He should have been far more successful.

Like Steven, he had a difficult mother. We all have our baggage to carry. He didn't have a good relationship with his mother as an adult because she smothered him, didn't give him a chance to breathe when he was younger. That had a lot to do with his lack of confidence. Call it selfish or jealous but I was happy she kept her distance. I wanted Bob to have nobody else but me.

Pamela, Alice and Barbara

He was a very good man and he was good to Alice and Pamela. He never said no to me. He told me that he wanted to make up for all the hard times I had lived through.

He was too good to some people and sometimes he was disappointed when he helped a young person or someone at work and they never thanked him or appreciated him. He did it because he was a giver and he enjoyed it.

I have guilt to this day because I didn't appreciate him. Everyone has been telling me through the decades—psychiatrists, therapists, etc.—that he enjoyed taking care of me, but still I regret my behavior. At times I even tried to put him down because I was so insecure.

Bob got his masters degree in business; he had an important position in a company. I didn't appreciate how smart he was. He left that job because they asked him to move to another city; he didn't want to relocate.

He also had a law degree but never took the bar exam. He went to work for the City of New York. He worked there with lawyers. I don't know what his title was but he loved it, a civil service job.

He read constantly. On the many bookshelves in our apartment, every book had little scraps of yellow paper sticking out where he had marked a significant passage or quote of interest. It was just amazing how he knew so many things. But he wasn't the type to sit around and read and cut the grass. He loved to work.

Dancing with Bob at our wedding

He retired from the city job but he couldn't stand idleness so he went back to work as a paralegal. That's when I talked him into going to rabbinical school. He wasn't the type to go exercising or just sit and read all day. He was one of those people who are only happy when they are busy and feeling productive.

Bob died on his way home from work, exactly as he had predicted. He went to work, had a full day, then had a heart attack in the elevator on his way home. I was alone as Alice lived in the group home, Barbara was in Chicago married and Pamela lived with her husband in Staten island. I was totally devastated.

Fortunately for me, I had a very good friend who had lost her sight twenty years before. She had gone to Florida for the winter. For three months she let me stay in her apartment in Washington Heights because I could go home only to get the mail. That's how I got over it.

After three months I gradually went back to my apartment but it was a very traumatic time for me. I was married to him the longest and he was very supportive of me. He had some issues, who doesn't? If you have parents or partners, you have issues. But he was a very giving man and I needed someone like that.

Bob's daughter, Karen, and I became totally estranged. After her father died, she never called, just totally disappeared. Maybe it was my fault because I had been jealous of her, not wanting to share Bob, but she never put in any effort to contact me or to bond with any of my daughters. In fact Barbara's husband in Chicago really liked Karen and her husband. When he came to New York, they all went out together, including Pamela and her husband.

I heard that Karen divorced her husband and moved to California but I don't know for sure. She had issues with her father but who doesn't have some conflict. Why is that? In every family there is always stuff.

I didn't want to marry Bob at first, but I was seeing my Jungian therapist at the time. He liked Bob and encouraged me to marry him. He thought Bob would be good for me. Bottom line, I married him even though I resisted. He was the kind who didn't let go and I needed that. He went after me.

It was very traumatic for me when he died, a more difficult time for me than when Steven died. I had been married to Steven for sixteen years, I had teenage children, I learned to drive. But it was harder for me when Bob died in October, 2000, right after I was ordained.

All three husbands had in common a desire to make me happy. Even the first, the bi-polar one, tried, and I certainly wasn't easy to be with or deal with. I could never say "I love this man" in any of my marriages.

I could never do that because I didn't want to be rejected. Men had to come after me.

People ask me how did I manage after all these losses. I love the movie, *Forest Gump*. I like to quote Forest when he said, "That was that." In each phase of my life, I tried to cope by not feeling, by saying to myself, "Well, that was that."

Raising a Down Syndrome Child

The major issue I encountered in having a Down Syndrome daughter was that I couldn't separate myself from her. She is considered "low functioning" but I always felt guilty that I didn't treat her more like my other daughters. I thought I was helping by doing everything for her, but I think she could have learned more if I had been different. She would have been much more independent, functioning at a higher level.

I feel for selfish reasons I kept her from developing more fully. I don't know how to explain it. I had so much remorse. I felt I had to do everything for her. She had a lot more potential, but because of the way I treated her, I kept her back. I froze her development.

She first went to a group home in Pennsylvania when she was eight years old. It was one of those schools that practiced a philosophy based on the beliefs of Rudolf Steiner. It was a very difficult time because I had the three girls and Alice kept beating up on Pamela. Of course, no matter what I did, Alice was smart enough to be jealous of Pamela and Pamela was jealous of her and all the attention I gave her.

I don't remember why but something happened at that home in Philadelphia and she had to leave. Now she is in the care of the Young Adult Institute in Scarsdale, New York, which sponsors many group homes for people like Alice. She lives closer to me. Before, it was a long way to get to Camp Hill, Pennsylvania. I remember it was a long drive, quite a few hours.

In the beginning, when Alice was school-age, I used to have her come home every weekend. Bob wasn't thrilled about that. He was very good to her but these visits were challenging. She displayed difficult behavior at times.

She also needed surgery for her heart because she was born with open ducts that had to be fixed. I remember her pediatrician suggested it was a philosophical question, whether it was a good thing to perform this surgery, but how could I not? Gradually the visits changed to twice a month until I got sick last year. Then I didn't see her for three months. Now she comes home about once a month. Before she comes, I always have great anxiety and fears about having her with me.

I still feel quite anxious when she comes even though she is very good now. She stays in my bedroom, I sleep on the sofa. It is a small apartment and I always wonder what to do with her. Most of the time she likes to stay in bed, listen to her music. It is easier, but it is not easy at the same time.

I pick her up and return her to Scarsdale, going by car service. Each time it is quite an expense. Lately the supervisor of the building offered to bring her to us, so it costs me for only one way.

I have so much guilt that it makes me anxious every day and even more so shortly before each time she comes to the apartment for a visit. For me that one day is like being in prison. I can't go to Zabar's or see people, I feel trapped. She must feel it too but in spite of my tension, she seems to like coming home.

So many people have told me to take a car service and just visit her there for a few hours. Acupuncturists, therapists and friends have all suggested this to me, but I don't feel right, not letting her "come home."

Relationship with Daughters

After the divorce, my first husband, Kurt, did not help in any way with Barbara. His family was not well off and I didn't have much to do with them, even though Kurt continued to give me many problems. He often came in the middle of the night to the apartment. Once, the doorman accidentally let him in.

When he was manic, he would call me and act like we were still married. I don't know what Barbara remembered about him but there is another part of her story that is so difficult to talk about. She didn't want to have much to do with her father because she was angry with him when, as a young adult, she was diagnosed with the same disease: Bi-polar Disorder, which caused us all so much suffering.

When Barbara was in graduate school, she continued to perform very well. She had inherited Kurt's musical talent. They both had an excellent ear. Kurt never had any formal training but could just sit down and play any piece. Barbara too was a gifted pianist.

At Juilliard she was very social and had a lot of friends. But then she started having mood swings that led to problems. The program was very intense and demanding and it became too much for her.

She left New York and went to graduate school in Chicago, after which she got a job and remained in the windy city. She majored in business administration so after graduation she went to work for the Ford Motor Company. She was coping while in graduate school, but when she started working and was under a lot of stress, her bipolar symptoms flared up. She worked for International Harvester after the Ford Company and again had a very stressful job.

She married someone, a non-Jew, from Chicago. Her illness was tough, she was hospitalized a few times. Her husband was very good to her. He really loved her.

After a number of years, she got a job with a small company and she liked it there. She was content and emotionally stable for awhile. Then the company went out of business and it was terrible for her. It was as if she lost her moorings, her sense of belonging. She couldn't find another job and was upset about her illness. She felt she was worthless, got more and more depressed, then was diagnosed with diabetes because she over-ate. She simply didn't take care of herself anymore.

Barbara died three years ago, ostensibly from complications of the diabetes. It was, according to my therapist, her choice, because she felt her mental illness kept her from realizing all the things she dreamed about doing.

My relationship with Barbara over the years was stormy at times. But still, she would call often, almost every day, and she would tell me personal things. Often mothers and daughters don't have a smooth relationship and ours was very erratic because of her illness.

At least she had her husband, he was her best friend. She complained about him sometimes, but they really loved each other. Her husband to this day still calls and keeps in touch with me. We have good conversations and he seems to care about me.

When Bob was alive and Alice lived in a home in Pennsylvania, we would visit her there—take her out for lunch, go for a ride, or do an activity and then take her back, but I can't do that now. I don't know what to do with her at the group home. Maybe it would be okay for Alice, but not for me.

So I continue to bring her home. I think it's not good enough if she doesn't stay one night. I do it for me, as I feel so guilty. I take her back in the morning so she can go to the day program that is part of her routine.

Pamela is now married and lives in Staten Island. She suffered a lot from having two sisters who were not well and having a mother like me. (How could she not suffer?) She experiences periods of depression and lacks self-confidence.

Pamela has a good job. She is still shy (she was always a quiet type of person), so she chose court stenography as a profession. It seemed to suit her personality. She is highly respected among her court colleagues.

Pamela for a long time didn't come to see Alice because, of course, she felt a lot of resentment. She always had some excuse why she couldn't come over, but she is getting a little better. She has even stayed overnight occasionally, sleeping on an inflatable bed because I give Alice my bed and I sleep on the couch. She has even offered to pay for the car service to bring Alice home, so she is changing a little.

I worry about Pamela a lot and regret that she has had so much to deal with. but I see her getting stronger emotionally and our relationship continues to improve. Pamela's and my relationship has had its ups and downs but I think I changed and she changed so things are much better between us.

Pamela's grandmother didn't come to visit very often so she didn't have a close relationship with her, her older sister died. Pamela's husband has no extended family. It is very sad, we have so little family.

I never talked about my experiences during the war, I kept it away from them. They never knew any details about my early childhood and incarceration at Auschwitz when they were children, but they felt it in the air. It is there, you don't have to say anything.

I have no grandchildren, a huge sadness for me as I love children.

Always Searching: Experiences with Therapy

I was always curious about the psyche even before I went into therapy. I used to talk with people, listen to their problems and maybe give them advice. They would look at me in surprise and ask, "Are you a therapist?" I don't know why I did that. Maybe that's why Kurt always told me I was a good actress.

During my marriage to Steven, we had a very active social life. He had many friends, and when they all married, we often socialized together every month. It was a very nice group of people. All those friends shared Steven's interests in music, jazz, and self-improvement. One of them, Stanley King, had a textile business designing fabrics.

Stanley knew my background and said to me one day, "I go to a therapist and I talk to him about you." (Here he is going to his session and talking about me!) "I really recommend that you go and see him." You know me, I try everything so that was all I had to hear.

Later I went to all kinds of therapy—past-life regression, even scream therapy—but this was my first therapeutic experience. I called Stanley's therapist, Dr. Steven Schwartz, but he wasn't taking new patients. He recommended another Jungian analyst whom he felt was perfect for me. He explained that Jonathan's family came from Germany; they too had to leave. That is how I ended up with this Jungian analyst with whom I have worked for forty-plus years, Jonathan Goldberg.

I call him Jonathan. After some individual sessions he recommended I would also benefit from a Jungian group that still meets. He saw me through the death of two husbands, the years of raising three daughters and now my own challenges as an older person.

I really feel bad saying anything negative about him because he is an extremely ethical person. When I got sick two years ago, he came to my apartment and stayed two hours without charging me. I was sick and he came to visit. So when I told him recently that I don't want to come every week anymore, it wasn't that I didn't want to see him. I was coming from a place of financial reality; I can't afford to see him weekly. He got upset and said that was not acceptable, that I need to continue on a regular basis.

I think this was the first time I stood up for myself and repeated that I will only be coming once a month. I had this resentment towards him because he thought I should leave my big apartment (maybe in hindsight he was right, but I loved that place where I had lived forty years). Then I see the other side because he went beyond the call of duty to visit me. I can see both sides so I feel guilty about holding these negative feelings.

The group has stayed together for the most part, eleven of us. A few people left over the years and new members joined. Not everybody was ready to hear stuff from other people; some couldn't handle it. In a very important way, this group has become my extended family and I continue to learn from them, to grow and feel nurtured.

Always curious to learn more, I have tried a lot of other therapeutic modalities in addition to my Jungian treatment. I tried every New Age approach there was. I was always a searcher, although I never knew what I was searching for.

In 1974 I attended some EST* sessions and then went to Lifespring, a take-off of EST. I learned a way to deal with fear in EST. The leader told me to imagine a dog is chasing me, it is biting at my heels. "Take the dog with you," the leader advised. "Take the dog with you." That is what I have learned to do.

I studied Reiki* and Past Life Regression,* where I had a vision of being chained. This image kept recurring every time I regressed under hypnosis to a previous life.

I worked with a physical therapist who told me my body was tight like a rock. She recommended I study the Alexander Technique.* After a period of Alexander work, she noted, "Your body is quite different now."

A massage therapist suggested I go to Omega, an organization based in Rhinebeck, New York, that offers a variety of workshops in a rustic camp-like setting. I attended a workshop titled "The Body Tells the Truth," led by a charismatic woman, Ilana Rubenfeld, who had created a body-mind approach to healing trauma—the Rubenfeld Synergy Method.* I was so affected by the workshop that I signed up for her training program.

She held the classes at her townhouse on Waverly Place in Greenwich Village, New York City where we met on a regular basis. I got to know a woman in the training group who was Ilana's favorite, but also became an important friend to me for many years, Kathryn Cunningham.

Although it is a very powerful method, at that time I still couldn't let out my feelings, so I didn't get the full benefit. I was no longer having flashbacks and I talked about my experiences during my childhood and the war very matter-of-factly. I held it together very well for many, many years.

Maybe that is why I had a breakdown last year. I do have nightmares sometimes now that I am in this Witness Theater program because it is all about the Holocaust. I wake up in terror, but it doesn't stay with me for long.

After graduating as a Rubenfeld Synergist in 1988, I had a small private practice in my home on 84th Street for several years. I liked meeting new clients and I was a good listener, but I wasn't comfortable with doing on-going work. I found it difficult if people came regularly. I had a couple of people who were very needy and it was draining.

Once I was a Certified Rubenfeld Synergist, I did go to Canada several times with Ilana to assist her, offering personal sessions to a new group of students. I stayed with a couple who had a whole group of people lined up for me to work with. Boy, was that tiring! I also personally wasn't ready to deal with my own locked up issues. So I kept searching while staying with my Jungian work.

*See Glossary at end for definitions.

Employment

Once Alice had moved to a residential setting when she was eight and Pamela had started school, I had a variety of jobs to contribute income and to keep myself busy. One day an osteopath saw something in me and advised, "You are the kind of personality who should move every five minutes—walk, jump, or move to get rid of all the stuff you are holding inside."

I worked in an electrical company as the "everything" person. I can never say, "I don't know how...," so I learned a variety of skills on the job, working there until the company went out of business.

I did some typing for a non-profit organization, then had a bookkeeping job, not knowing the difference at first between debit and credit.

I also worked as a volunteer at a nearby Jewish-run thrift shop. I liked being there because my job was to check in new items, so I got to pick the best selections for myself. The manager liked me and gave me an even better price.

When I see something I want to do, I make it happen. After a while I got to know a very nice man who suggested I start my own business. He offered to help me get started with a booth at the flea market on the corner of 26th Street and 6th Avenue. It was an empty lot filled with booths on Sundays.

For several years Bob helped me run a business there. Barbara and Pamela never offered to help and I never asked them. It never occurred to me. Maybe it was the culture or maybe I just have a hard time asking anyone to do anything for me.

It started with my bringing one item to a friend's booth on consignment where it sold right away. I was able to purchase clothes and accessories from the thrift shop at a very good price and add other items donated by friends or acquaintances to resell at the market. One woman was moving to India and brought a lot of her jewelry and clothing for me to sell.

It was extremely hard work. Bob and I got up at Three A.M. every Sunday in good weather. We hired a man with a station wagon to pick us up with all our boxes, drive us downtown and come back at the end of the day.

Bob was a great schmoozer, which brought us lots of customers. We met a lot of interesting people. Actors and politicians shopped, including Diane Keaton who loved our blankets. She stopped by almost every week.

The worst thing that happened once or twice a season was the onslaught from a sudden thunderstorm. We would have to stay there until our ride returned, so we attempted to cover the ware with tarps, but the wind and rain got through and wreaked havoc with our merchandise. Somehow we managed to pack it up and be right back there the next week.

I had to have eyes everywhere, as inevitably some people stole the best items when you looked away or were engaged with another customer, but overall it was profitable. People seemed to like my taste. My style is simple—some color, but elegant. Maybe because of the camps and financial struggles, I learned to make beauty out of very little. I have no patience for expensive or cluttered or frilly looks. My homes, my personal outfits are pleasing but simple and straightforward. I only sold what I would have liked for myself.

Becoming a Rabbi

I sent my husband, Bob Feller, to become a rabbi. After he retired, he went to work as a paralegal because he wasn't the kind of person who could relax or sit around. He had a law degree but he never took the Bar exam. Then he retired again; and again, he just had to work.

When we were looking for a rabbi to perform an interfaith wedding ceremony for Barbara, I had heard through word of mouth, through friends of Pamela's, about a Rabbi Gelberman. He had married Barbara and her non-Jewish husband, then later also married Pamela.

My ordination

Through conversations with the young couples and their friends, I learned about the rabbi's school where he offered courses to become a reverend or a rabbi. A non-Jewish friend of Pamela's studied with him and found it very helpful in her job and her personal life, so I thought it sounded as if it would be good for my husband to study there and keep busy.

He enrolled, he loved it, and eventually became a reverend. Then when the school offered a course to become a rabbi, he signed up. He was a natural. He started doing weddings. Couples would come to the house where he interviewed them before the ceremony. When he went to the weddings, I went along and I liked it. I always enjoyed doing new things. So I thought to myself, maybe I should take the course to become a rabbi too.

We met one day a week, about ten in the class, at the Rabbi's apartment very close to where I live now. He assigned a lot of work that we did on our own between classes, many readings and homework assignments. I also worked with a Jewish organization, AISH, that offers free classes so I studied as much and wherever I could. Volunteers would teach you whatever you wanted to learn, to read or write Hebrew for example, because we didn't get much of that from the rabbi. I even studied at night with a lovely very Orthodox woman.

Studying the most important prayer in Judaism, the Shema (recited in the morning and evening to express faith in and love of God) helped me start to reclaim my Jewish identity. After all my studying, I passed the test. I had to write a service and do all kinds of projects. I can read biblical Hebrew but I can't read a Ketubah, the traditional wedding contract. Recently I performed a ceremony and the Ketubah was written in Aramaic. I couldn't fill it out since I couldn't read it. I gave it to Israeli friends and even they couldn't read it.

to acknowledge her Jewish identity to hundreds of people. At this hour of religious fanaticism, Renée Feller casts bridges between different cultures and confessional differences. The future wedded couples belong to different cultures but their traditions blend. She has married a Hindu and a Jew.

"Renée notes, 'These religions join each other. In a Jewish marriage, a tent is erected, called the chuppah, open on four sides to symbolize that their home will be welcoming to all. The fiancee turns around her future husband seven times. The gesture symbolizes protection. In Hinduism the couple unites under the Mandapa which symbolizes the home/hearth they will build. They then turn seven times around the hearth/fire.'

"Renée, accompanied by a priest, also united a Jew and a Zoroastrian. To respect the Zoroastrian tradition, she and the priest placed on the table seven spices, including the poppy seeds and salt, which protect against the evil eye. They also placed a needle and thread.

"'According to Zoroastrian tradition,' said Renée with an amused smile, 'the needle and thread will be used to sew shut the mouth of the mother-in-law.'

"Even if the couple is not practicing their religion, they like to feel that they are participating in their cultural traditions when they marry.

"'Which is why I research the traditions that speak to the future couple,' continued Renée. 'According to a Jewish tradition, they say that forty days before the birth of a child, its husband or wife is chosen in heaven. These two souls, if they find each other on earth, will fall in love and become one. A Chinese legend says nearly the same. A couple is already aligned at birth by an invisible red thread which continues to shrink until the couple is wed.'

"One day Renée wed a Sikh and a Hindu. After searching in vain for someone ready to celebrate an inter-religious marriage, the future couple came across her website. After presiding over the ceremony, Renée was complimented by the father of the bride. 'In thirty minutes, what we have experienced here was stronger than what we experienced in four days in India.'

"Sometimes she had to force herself to accept a request to officiate at a marriage. 'A couple wanted an inter-religious marriage in Germany. The fiancé was Jewish and had invited about twenty of his American family for the wedding. The fiancee was Christian. I was afraid to go there. It was the first time since the Holocaust that I'd been in a country that tortured me. It was very moving and mending, both for me as well as for the second generation of Germans present. I came back from Germany telling myself that it's impossible to be driven by hate.'

"Inter-religious marriages are still somewhat exceptional. The resistance remains strong. Renée doesn't celebrate the marriages in synagogues. She allows the couple to choose their marriage site-along a river, at a university campus.

"To find an Imam who will agree to an inter-religious marriage is not easy. Islam tends to be stricter in this regard. Nevertheless the New Yorker has found an Imam from Turkey, living in Manhattan, who is willing-with her-to unite a Jew and a Muslim in marriage.

"Parents are often the stumbling block. For the marriage of a Catholic and a Jew in the outskirts of Paris, the parents of the groom refused to attend. For them, celebrating the marriage in a church was unacceptable.

"'You often need lots of psychology,' acknowledges Renée. 'But it's important to know what the couple wants. If their wishes are clear, the parents generally follow. If that's not the case, it's often necessary to await the arrival of the babies for the grandparents to come around.'

"Before the wedding, the rabbi usually gives the couple a marriage project that includes expressing the wishes of each. This could even include questions about children. In what religion will they be raised?

"'It depends,' explains Rabbi Renée. 'If one of the couple is more religious than the other, it's often that parent who will determine the religion of the *children. But often, the parents are creative. For example, A Jew and a Catholic decided that if the child is a boy, he'd be raised as a Jew, if a girl, she'd be raised as a Catholic.'*

"Reconciled with the Divine, Renée Feller developed her strategy: recover from the wounds of inhumanity by opening to the world. Without reservation. It is in this spirit that she went recently to celebrate a gay marriage at Sitges, near Barcelona.

"'I love these people. I love to learn about them. Without judging them,' she said. 'A powerful lesson in humanity.'"

Officiating at a wedding

I loved doing this wedding for the gay couple. I love those two guys and have known them for years. They have recommended me to many of their friends and relatives. My friend, Catherine, told me not to go, saying I was not the person I used to be, after the breakdown I had had. She felt I could no longer travel as I used to do. I was a little nervous about it, I was still recovering, but I was determined to go and when I determine I want to do something, I do it. Actually it worked out very well.

That was the first time ever that I went against Catherine's advice or anyone else's for that matter. My therapist said, "If you do go, you should take Pamela with you," which I decided not to do. I had all these opinions from others about how to live my life, but, for one of the first times in my eighty-five years, I listened to my own instincts. It turned out to be an easy trip, a six-hour flight. My gay friends were super generous, picking me up and taking me around.

I did other weddings and had some wonderful experiences. For a couple of years I went very often to Europe—twice to Germany, to Italy, France, Switzerland—also to Mexico and Puerto Rico. I did a lot of destination weddings. It was very exciting. Some people were super generous, others were on the cheap side, but I loved each occasion.

I was always ready to go, but always with fear. I took the fear with me, the coping skill I learned at EST. I imagine that I have a dog barking at my heels, then I take that dog with me.

Couples come to see me several times before the wedding. (I learned from my own therapy just to listen). In our meetings I ask them how they met, how friendship became love. I would write all that down. I would sometimes see issues. If they asked me, I would recommend things they could do, such as examine the teachings of Buddhism. I would quote from Buddhist scriptures and talk about accepting.

Then during the wedding I speak for seven to ten minutes, especially looking for some funny stories. I always give a homily, which is a presentation of the rabbi's personal remarks. I don't say the same thing each time because I base my commentary on what I learn from the couple that is interesting to me. Everyone seems to approve. But that part is the hardest for me as I wait until the last minute so it is fresh.

One of my favorite weddings involved a gorgeous couple. He was a surgeon at the Hospital for Special Surgery. The reason the bride chose me, after looking for a rabbi on the Internet, was because I was a Holocaust survivor. Interesting, no? Especially because she was a Christian girl from the Midwest. When I asked them how they met, they said it was a very boring story but I encouraged her to tell me anyhow.

She went to a bar on the Upper East Side where he spotted her. He asked her what she did and she didn't want to tell him she was a model because he might think she wasn't very smart, so she told him she was a medical student. He started to ask her questions about where she was training and what she was learning. Of course she couldn't answer. If she had known he was a doctor, she would have made up a different occupation. But they were attracted to one another and, in spite of her initial story, they eventually got married.

After performing a wedding ceremony

I made it into a very funny story and people came up to me after the ceremony and said I should become an actor, I was so good. That is not the first time people have told me that. I think in my past life I was an actress because I enjoy being on stage.

For much of my life I didn't want to acknowledge my Jewishness. I was always hiding. Maybe becoming a rabbi was my way of owning my Jewishness for the first time. Actually it has been only in the last few years, that when somebody asks me, "What is your religion?" I can answer, "I am Jewish." Before it was very difficult to even say the word.

So when I started doing weddings, there I was in front of a crowd. I didn't consciously understand my need to claim my heritage. It came up one day in my Jungian group when I mentioned that I feel so good when I do a wedding. I feel another layer peeling off. This is why the group is good, why I continue to go to meetings. The group consists mostly of therapists plus a few other professionals, but it is very important to me, like a family.

Moving Up, Moving On

How I got to my current apartment is a long story. When I was married to my third husband, Bob, it seemed inevitable to move to 86th street. (I had always wanted to live on the Upper West Side. When I lived in Inwood, I dreamed of living in this area.) So we found an apartment on 86th Street between Columbus and Central Park West and I lived there for forty years. It was big, a beautiful apartment, everyone was jealous. And then, in October, 2013 I had a breakdown. That's what my doctor called it because no one could figure out what else it could be.

One day, maybe it was more than one day, I couldn't make myself get out of bed, I felt so sick. I didn't know that I had pneumonia because I didn't cough or have a fever. A friend of mine, Kathryn, called me, just a coincidence. If she hadn't called me, I don't know what would have happened. She said in a concerned voice, "You don't sound like yourself."

I can really thank her because she came over. I was confused, I was lying in bed and couldn't get up, couldn't get up to feed the cat. So my friend called an ambulance which took me to the hospital where they found I had pneumonia.

I was in the hospital for three days, that was it, and then they sent me home. My doctor said even though I was okay, I should have someone with me for a few days. I shouldn't be alone. So I found somebody through this friend (who doesn't speak to me now, but that is another story) and I thought I was okay, just a little shaky.

The aide and I went for a walk and I wasn't paying attention. I fell on the sidewalk. I didn't break anything, but I really hurt myself. From that point on, I started having tremendous anxiety, I was afraid to be alone. I fell more than once. One time I got a glass of water and the water spilled so I slipped. I had a cab run into me. I had all these incidents and I had trouble walking. Out of nowhere my balance was terrible.

I had an aide with me for several months. My doctor sent me for every test, but they found absolutely nothing medically wrong. Kathryn was very helpful. She told me what to do, and I wanted, needed someone to tell me what to do. Why didn't I say what I wanted? I just didn't. Everyone thought I should move, even my therapist said my place was too big to live there alone, I was too anxious.

I went to see a famous neurologist, after waiting months for an appointment. She studied her computer. (That's what all the doctors do now, they look at their computer). Finally she said the problem was that my sodium was too low. But I still had a lot of problems. I had to use a walker. When I think back, I realize that I was afraid to walk.

Everyone thought the best thing to do was to go to an assisted living facility. I agreed because I was afraid to be alone. I couldn't wait to go. I said I don't need this woman anymore. (It was a tremendous amount of money out of pocket.)

My friends and my daughter looked for places and decided I should go to the Hebrew Home in Riverdale, New York. It was the nicest of all the places they had looked at but still I never really advocated for myself.

A woman came from Riverdale and told me what to bring with me, what to sell, what to get rid of. I had a tremendous number of things that one accumulates over time. So I gave up my big apartment that I loved and moved to Riverdale.

By then I could walk, I had recovered, but I was miserable there. I couldn't stand it. It reminded me of the Holocaust, the people standing in line. Not that you *had* to stand in line but the people would line up before meals with their walkers. I thought I would die.

I was there about two months when I heard of a place on the Upper East Side called Carnegie East, and I thought, at least I would be back in Manhattan. So I moved from Riverdale to 94th Street on the Upper East Side but I still wasn't happy. I couldn't stay there so after four months, I moved back to Riverdale. I had to do what I had to do, otherwise I would go out of my mind.

A young man came to offer activities at Riverdale. Sometimes after classes he would sit at our table and dine with us. After he got to know me, he said one day, "What are you doing here? You don't belong here." He had a lot to do with my coming back to the Upper West Side, to 104th Street, to my own apartment.

Every time I moved I left a little more behind. I sold or gave away all of my rugs. I needed window treatments and other things so I learned how to buy on Amazon. Imagine all this moving back and forth at my age, it's insane. But I must say, everywhere I went, they wanted me back!

As did many survivors, I thought I was doing the right thing, not telling the children anything about my background or the Holocaust. They felt it in the air, they have the leftovers, the feelings, even though I didn't say anything about those years.

I married Jewish men but they didn't really care about participating in religious observances. My daughters didn't go to Hebrew school. We didn't belong to a synagogue but we did have the rituals, the holiday dinners. Bob was very Jewish in his heart but did nothing outwardly.

I didn't believe in formal religion. I didn't give Barbara or Pamela any Jewish training so they didn't grow up feeling Jewish. Even to this day, I don't have any feeling for religious services but I do love the music. I would go to any synagogue—reform, orthodox, wherever—to hear beautiful music. That's what moves me, not the words about God.

That would be hypocritical. Someone recently sent me a Rosh Hashanah card with a tape from You Tube, Barbara Streisand singing Aveinu Malkeinu, the prayer of forgiveness. I just loved it. It moved me to tears as does any cantorial singing. Ordinary prayers don't do anything for me

Living Now

Dr. Patricia Boyle, a neuropsychologist and researcher at the Rush Alzheimer's Disease Center, a part of Rush Medical Center in Chicago, has been studying what helps older people defer illness and dementia. She proposes a concept of "reserve," borrowed from physiology.

Most systems in our bodies are able to sustain some level of damage before they start to malfunction. Having a purpose in life may not slow the formation of plaques and tangles in the brain, but it appears to increase the reserve that the brain calls on before it stars to break down, perhaps by spurring other healthy brain connections that compensate for the decline. The stronger the purpose, the more is added to the reserve.

So that is one thing that saves me. I suffer from depression and anxiety, I have it all the time, but I am interested in new things and people. I go to Zabar's almost every morning where I meet very interesting people, which is energizing and wonderful for me. One crowd comes in the morning, and in the afternoon come the senior citizens. I have no patience for the things they talk about and I don't identify with being old.

In the morning, however, I talk with all kinds of people (not just men, because I am not looking for a man). For instance, there is a Chinese man who is a retired professor of engineering from Columbia University. His wife died a year ago. I am learning from him about a different culture, Chinese history. He is just one example. I find all these conversations very stimulating.

Recently I was invited to participate in a weekly program offered by a non-profit group. The organization, Witness Theater, selected ten interested high school students from two New York City schools, Abraham Heschel and Trinity, to meet with six Holocaust survivors. The program runs for eight months in two-hour sessions during which the students interview us about our experiences during World War II.

At the end, the students will act out the survivors' stories, which they weave into a play that will be performed in the spring. When I first walked into the room and began talking to these young people, so eager to hear my challenges of survival, I was choked with emotion.

The kids give me so much attention; they admire who I am. There are eight girls and two boys; half of them are Jewish. One girl who is Irish plays my Inner Self while another girl who is Jewish plays the part of my Outer Self. The girls are always admiring my clothes and jewelry, asking me where I bought whatever I am wearing. They seem to think I am a pretty hip lady at my age. Once they asked me where I shop, and I told them Uniqlo (a Japanese owned clothing franchise geared towards a young market), they couldn't imagine anyone my age shopping there.

The guys treat me like royalty. They surround me and want to join me, to come with me to my Tai Chi class, sit with me at Zabar's. Everything I wear—the earrings, the clothes—they make a big deal about because I am not like some of the other adults in their lives. It is the sweetest thing. It is very flattering and makes me feel young! And it's fun.

I didn't get this kind of appreciation from my own daughters. They didn't admire me or give me any compliments. So for me this experience is very gratifying. I also get admiration from the people in charge, from the drama teacher and the whole team. It inspires me.

When I come home from exercise class on Tuesdays, I am tired. I wish I could stay home but I have to go to this class. I am kind of obsessive, so if that is my regular routine, I don't want to give it up. I want to say to myself, it's Tuesday so I don't have to go to the gym because I will be tired later for Witness Theater, but I can't. Not me. I have to go to the gym, I have to go to the program. I want to do it all!!

Another lucky thing for me is that I am always eager to learn new things. Not as much as when I was younger; then I overdid it. I always enjoyed exercise; being physical is very important for my mental state. Much more than reading, as reading requires you to be still. Sitting still is not for me. I do read books but I don't devour them like I used to. I love Tai Chi as it is very quieting for the mind.

For decades I did weights and swimming and all kinds of activities. Then someone told me about a great ballet class so I tried it. Now I am hooked, even though I have pain in my hips. Ballet is not easy. It is a different kind of movement, and it is good for me because it is new. I don't care that I leave there in pain. (Medicine doesn't help me. I have tried so many, and so many supplements and vitamins, for decades, and I don't feel they made a difference).

Someone who believes in astrology talks about my being a Leo. This woman, who is an artist, said people are drawn to me. When I go to Zabar's in the mornings, I want to just sit and be quiet, but the minute I arrive, people are coming over and talking to me. I don't know what this is about me. Maybe I give off an energy that says to others that I love people, I love to learn.

I have two layers, one that craves privacy and space and is fear-based, the other that seeks people and connection and adventure. Years ago someone told me that my Jungian archetype is to draw people to me. I didn't realize this for decades. It's wonderful that I am still learning, going deeper and deeper inside.

When my daughters were growing up, I started my day, after sending them off to school, by going to a coffee shop. I had my favorites and I always sat in the window looking out. I didn't want to talk to anyone; I just needed to be among people, that was my routine.

Over many years and a lot of working on myself, plus life experiences, I went from sitting near the window, not wanting to talk to anyone to the present, going to Zabar's, sitting in the middle of the communal table where you can't help but talk to others and soak up connections with others.

Every morning when I first wake up, I am terrified, filled with free-floating anxiety. I worry about dying because I worry what will happen to Alice and Pamela. And I worry about becoming incapacitated again, ill and dependent on others. Then I push myself, refocus, get up and start moving.

I take the bus twenty blocks to Zabar's, usually four times a week, where I always meet fascinating people and learn something new. Then I go to a Tai Chi or exercise class three times a week in Greenwich Village, and then to a different coffee shop for a change. It is very helpful to me to keep doing; it takes me away from depression.

It's amazing how I went from not wanting to talk to anyone, sitting in a corner of a coffee shop, to enjoying meeting new people, learning about their lives and cultures. I am loving my world, until evening when quiet returns and once again I face my demons.

Reflecting on my past, I think I was born with an inner strength that has allowed me to survive all these years, to believe that I can go on, that I will not fall apart. All those decades I was able to hold it together until two years ago when I couldn't anymore. It has a lot to do with your genes, this survival instinct. Maybe I have done more than survive.

Every day it is difficult for me to get up, every day it is a challenge. But I do it. I would much rather stay in bed and pull the covers over my head, but then I would feel terrible. I know it would not be good for me. Getting involved is key, a biggie. That is what keeps me going. The secret is in the doing. That is the thing, to feel the depression and keep going in spite of it, to "take your dog with you, biting at your heels."

I have peeled off layers of rejection, of hurt and fear and trauma, the denial of my Jewishness, the denial of feelings and of my very soul, to now, a time where I embrace life, where I am thriving.

At last, I celebrate myself!

L'Chaim! To life!

ADDENDUM I

Witness Theater 2016

The memories of Holocaust survivors often die with them, but now an unusual program is helping to give their experiences new life onstage. Witness Theater, introduced in New York City in 2012 by Selfhelp Community Services, a Jewish aid organization, pairs Holocaust survivors with high school students who work together to create a dramatic production. Over a period of many months, the survivors met with the students and shared their memories.

The students, with the help of their director, Jenny Velarde-Ragan, pieced together those stories and created six short plays. Those who experienced the Holocaust served as narrators, while their young collaborators re-enacted incidents from the survivors' lives. The results were staged in May at several different locations.

The script was created by Students of Trinity and Abraham Heschel High Schools, New York City, New York, 2016. Renée Feller narrated as ADULT RENÉE. Her inner self, represented by RENEÉ, and her outer self, RENEÉ #1 are played by two students, one Jewish and one Christian. Smaller parts are enacted by other students.

Renée's Story

ADULT RENEÉ: I am an Ordained Rabbi who does Interfaith weddings. There isn't a member of a religion that I haven't married in connection with a Jewish person. I accept people the way they are. I've always been interested in other people and other cultures. In the beginning it was very scary because I was being seen by hundreds of people, but I did it. On the outside I looked strong but on the inside I felt scared. When I feel scared, I take my fear and carry it with me. I have no idea where I learned this, but I think I've been doing it my whole life.

RENEÉ: There were many times in my childhood that I felt terrified, but I didn't show fear. On the inside I felt one thing. But on the outside I presented another way. I had a way of covering up. Maybe I was born this way. (*Photo shown*) Maybe it was a gift. In any case, it saved my life. I am from Hungary, the Carpathian Mountain area.

RENEÉ #1: Where people came for skiing and our well-known natural spring water.

RENEÉ: It was a small town. There was only one synagogue. It was orthodox.

RENEÉ #1: Upstairs for the women, and downstairs for the men.

RENEÉ: My family owned two bakeries, the only ones in town.

RENEÉ #1: We were the bakers.

RENEÉ: (*Photo shown*) My mother was the glamorous type. I had a younger brother. I was very protective of him. No one could beat him up. No one could say a bad word about him.

RENEÉ #1: Except me, of course. (*Nudges brother*)

RENEÉ: My mother died when I was six years old. This was so hard (*turning to RENEÉ #1*) but I don't show it. My father married my mother's cousin.

RENEÉ #1: (*To RENEÉ*) I'm not happy about this. I think she's stupid.

ADULT RENEÉ: If I knew then, what I know now, I would be able to see why I didn't like her. She was actually a decent woman.

RENEÉ: That's true. (*Nods and smiles to ADULT RENEÉ. RENEÉ #1 is frowning.*) We didn't have fancy toys.

RENEÉ #1: I never had a doll.

RENEÉ: But I remember I loved using my imagination and playing in nature. The garden. The beautiful mountains.

RENEÉ #1: Playing in the dirt. Gooseberries in the bushes. Running up the hill with a bucket to collect our famous water.

RENEÉ: The adults never talked to me about the impending war, but by eight years old I could feel there was something going on.

RENEÉ #1: I can hear them whispering.

RENEÉ: The first incident. Hungarian authorities were collaborating with the Nazis. My father, brother and I were taken to a ghetto because my father's papers were not in order. We weren't the only ones, but I can't recall seeing anyone else. We stayed there for weeks but I don't remember details. I do recall sleeping on the floor, on hay. For me, it's always been important that my surroundings look the best they can.

RENEÉ #1: I tried to decorate my little area on the floor.

RENEÉ: Though it felt like a haze, it was a very strong feeling inside. Being taken away from my home for the first time. Not knowing when or if I ever would go back home again.

ADULT RENEÉ: Fear!

RENEÉ: (*Nodding to ADULT RENEÉ*) This was the real beginning. We returned home, though soon, they were collecting men for forced labor. My father fled to Budapest and left us alone with our cousin, or rather, our new stepmother.

RENEÉ #1: He left us with her.

RENEÉ: I know. It was 1944. Passover. All the Jewish people of the town were told to gather in a big field outside of town.

RENEÉ #1: We can bring our feather beds. And toothbrushes.

RENEÉ: We didn't know where we were going or how long we would be gone. Everybody thought we were just going for a little outing and would be back.

RENEÉ #1: I can hear rumors. People are hiding their jewelry in toothpaste.

RENEÉ: But I was always very quiet.

ADULT RENEÉ: I was always a listener.

(*RENEÉ #1 lying in the field. Quiet and stoic.*)

RENEÉ: We were in those fields for who knows how many days.

RENEÉ #1: Then they took everything away from us.

RENEÉ: And if I saw something cruel, I would pretend I didn't. That was my survival mechanism.

RENEÉ #1: We went to the railroad station. There were cattle trains. The young people climbed up, but the older people had to be helped into those trains. I remember seeing my eighty-nine year old grandmother being lifted up into a different car by two officers.

(RENEÉ #1 standing, not moving, or blinking.)

RENEÉ: Crowded, no air, no light, no sitting, no sleeping. Who knows how many weeks. My brother? My stepmother? I can remember many things but I do not recall what happened in that train.

ADULT RENEÉ: It's amazing. When something is so horrible, your unconscious mind doesn't want you to remember.

RENEÉ: Finally, the trains stopped. Nazis were there to greet us along with the Polish people, helping them. I remember Right. And the Left. While I was standing there, I remember a man said to me…

RENEÉ #1: When it came my turn, say you are older.

NAZI: State your age.

RENEÉ #1: I'm eighteen.

RENEÉ: I used my instinct. I lied, I made myself five years older.

NAZI: Go to the Left.

ADULT RENEÉ: That saved my life.

RENEÉ: But my brother, I couldn't save him. He was too young. He had to go to the other side. I couldn't do anything about it, but even to this day, I feel guilty.

(Moment of reflection)

RENEÉ: The next thing I knew, we arrived to the entrance gates with a big sign: Arbeit Macht Frei. "Work Makes You Free." We had arrived to

RENEÉ #1: Auschwitz. *(Pointing things out to RENEÉ)* There was a live band playing music. There were tables set up and the Germans meticulously registered every person.

NAZI: State your name, please.

RENEÉ: The feeling was that they didn't want to scare us. They didn't want panic. They made us feel as if we were on a holiday.

RENEÉ #1: Then they shaved our hair.

RENEÉ: They took away all our clothes and put on striped uniforms. A long striped dress. They stripped not just our clothes but our dignity and everything else.

ADULT RENEÉ: Even as a young girl I knew this.

RENEÉ: I remember being taken to the barracks. They had things like bunk beds. Three levels, but not for one person and it wasn't a bed. Just wood, no blankets. We were on the top. I was huddled together with my cousins and other strangers. That's where we slept and ate.

RENEÉ #1: There are *worms* in the soup.

STEPMOTHER: Here, eat my bread.

RENEÉ: It all felt like a fog. My brother. Everyone else. It was as if they faded into the background and they didn't exist anymore. The only thought I could think was.....

RENEÉ, RENEÉ #1, ADULT RENEÉ: Survive.

(Long pause. RENEÉ #! standing on stage, still.)

NAZI: Line up!

RENEÉ: When you were in Auschwitz they were always selecting people who looked sick or weak. I always tried to look strong and healthy.

ADULT RENEÉ: It's amazing that even after seventy years I cannot allow myself to feel tired or exhausted. I have to keep going. I have to keep strong.

RENEÉ: One day they were doing selections again from a group of women. I was crying *(RENEÉ #! crying)* because I was frightened. My eyes were red because of it.

NAZI: Are you sick?

RENEÉ #1: No. I'm not sick.

NAZI: Come!

RENEÉ: But he still pulled me out of this group and put me in the other.

RENEÉ #1:To *(RENEÉ, pointing to the other group)* That group is strong.

RENEÉ: I knew instinctively that this group was headed for the gas chamber. They didn't think I was strong enough. There were guards everywhere. I remember knowing I had to get out of that group. So I ran and went back to the one I came from.

(RENEÉ #! runs back to the other group.)

RENEÉ #!: (Whispering) I did it!

RENEÉ: The guard didn't catch me.

STEPMOTHER: You're back!

RENEÉ: They thought they would never see me again. I found my way back to the living.

ADULT RENEÉ: I did what I had to do.

RENEÉ: I was at Auschwitz for…

RENEÉ #!: Four months.

RENEÉ: Then, they were choosing again. This time I wasn't crying. *(RENEÉ #! stands strong)* This time I was put with the living. We were sent away to work in an ammunition factory. Every morning we would march through the town to the factory.

RENEÉ #!: We leave at 6 am and come back at 6 pm. Twelve hour shifts.

RENEÉ: What's interesting was I don't remember seeing people on the streets, but I do remember very clearly how amazed I was because there was feather bedding airing in the windows. There were all these windows with down covers. I would say to my cousin…

RENEÉ #1: *(Whispering)* There are actually people living like normal?!

ADULT RENEÉ: I thought everybody lived like we did.

RENEÉ #1: This food is terrible.

RENEÉ: I remember my greatest wish at the time. We were so starved that potato peels were a luxury item to us. My wish was that I could eat as many potato peels that I ever wanted when I got out. I didn't wish for a steak or shrimp. I wished for

RENEÉ #1: Potato peels.

RENEÉ: We were sitting around a big table assembling machine guns. The people that ran the factories were older men. Too old to be soldiers. I remember one day.

MAN: Shhh. *(Puts pears in laps of RENEÉ #1, COUSIN, and STEPMOTHER)*

RENEÉ: He had secretly brought us pears from his garden. I will never forget it.

ADULT RENEÉ: This was one of the kindest things I've ever experienced.

COUSIN: *(Whispering)* The Americans are coming.

STEPMOTHER: *(Whispering)* The Russians too.

RENEÉ: When the Germans realized they were losing, they herded us onto a train. I didn't know where they were taking us or what their plan was. Finally the Americans came on the trains to free us. Allied soldiers were coming towards the Nazis who had their hands up in surrender. The Nazis were forced to give up. They were no match.

RENEÉ #1: *(To COUSIN and STEPMOTHER)* We are free?

RENEÉ: We are no longer under the Germans.

RENEÉ #1: We are free.

RENEÉ: But there was total disorder. Things were chaotic. The former prisoners were breaking into factories and stealing things. We didn't know where to go or what to do. I couldn't go back home. We were nowhere for a while.

ADULT RENEÉ: We were so traumatized that our wish was to be back under some control.

RENEÉ: We ended up staying in an abandoned home. In the meantime the Federation for Jewish Philantropies was involved in connecting families to people in the United States.

RENEÉ #1: I have an uncle?

RENEÉ: My mother's oldest brother arranged for my papers. I waited for weeks. In the meantime we found another deserted home in Prague. The beds were infested with bed bugs. They would eat you alive. It was so bad....

RENEÉ #1: I slept on the kitchen table.

RENEÉ: I don't know how I came up with this stuff. I was practical.

RENEÉ #1: The bugs won't be on the kitchen table!

RENEÉ: Soon I was on a boat headed to New York. Even with all the work I have done through years of self-exploration, some memories are buried so deeply that I just cant remember. It's interesting what a human being can....

RENEÉ #1: Endure.

RENEÉ: Endure.

ADULT RENEÉ: Endure.

RENEÉ: It's really amazing to think about. It's incredible.

ADULT RENEÉ: Fifteen years now I've been a Rabbi. I've married many people throughout the years. Once I officiated at a wedding in Germany. It was fifty years after the Holocaust. To be honest, I was scared to death to go. Yet, I did. The German crowd had never seen a woman Rabbi before. During the service, it was very interesting, because everyone in the crowd was crying. Many people shared with me after the ceremony that it was very moving to have me there. They were grateful to me and were amazed I would come to Germany to do this. For me, it was a very healing experience. It was an experience I could never have had without forgiveness, without acceptance, and without carrying my fear with me.

ADDENDUM II

Wedding Homily by Rabbi Renée Feller

There is a saying that God continually creates new worlds by causing marriages take place. This is the beginning of your new world, and the beginning that the two of you are making. It is in the dawn of its creation. And God is saying. "It is good." Just like he did in Genesis. Together you are healing each other, balancing each other, filling in each other's gaps.

Thomas Merton, a theologian wrote: "Love is our true destiny, we do not find the meaning of life by ourselves alone, we find it with one another." Jenny and Peter have certainly found the meaning of life with each other.

They met in Munich in March 2008 when Jenny, an American and Jewish, was on a business trip and Peter was on his way home from his first proper vacation in years, a ski trip in Austria. While the rest of his group decided to drive home directly, Peter preferred to detour through Munich to see a Rothko exhibit and have dinner at a favorite restaurant, "Spatenhaus." Jenny's brother Joseph, who had traveled through Munich for the World Cup in 2006, recommended the same restaurant to his sister on her first night in Germany. Jenny doesn't remember that Peter held the door for her as she entered the restaurant, and thought she was Spanish. (Jenny thinks that's a compliment.)

Both on their own were seated at a communal table. When the many plates of food began to arrive, Peter sensed that Jenny was slightly overwhelmed and felt obligated to relate that portion sizes are unusually large in Bavaria and that one was certainly not expected to eat everything. Jenny was less overwhelmed than exhausted, jetlagged from a redeye flight and the time difference. However, once the conversation started, she began to get her energy back.

They immediately talked easily over a span of topics like art and architecture, food and traveling. After dinner, Peter suggested heading to a nearby café, where they discovered a shared love of whiskey and continued talking without effort.

Towards the end of the evening Jenny asked about recommendations for Berlin, as her business trip would end with a long weekend of sightseeing in the German capital and she'd been so busy with work she hadn't made any plans. Peter immediately offered to meet her there and show her around, as he knew the city well. However, he was careful to state that he did not want to intrude on her vacation. He drove the seven hours home to Hagen. The next day he called Jenny.

They ended up talking every day of the week and a half until they met up again in Berlin. Jenny's brother was also in Berlin that weekend, and met Peter, which set the pace for how fast things were going to move in the relationship. Over the course of the weekend, things quickly became serious and "the rest is history." Jenny reminds Peter that good things happen on vacations.

Both love food, so they often joke that it's probably no accident that they met in a restaurant. Jenny feels that Peter's Munich trip sums up his character perfectly—he took an overnight detour by himself, to see great art and eat great food. How could she not fall in love with a man like that?

Jenny and Peter's relationship developed into a kind of love neither of them had known before. They bring out the best in each other. They appreciate and cherish each other's uniqueness and honor that individuality. They communicate well. They are kind, caring, and compassionate people and share a wonderful sense of humor. They love each other unconditionally. They are best friends and soul mates.

I would like to read excerpts from selections of the mystical poems by the poet Rumi. "The minute I heard my first love story, I started looking for you, not knowing how blind I was." "Lovers don't finally meet somewhere. They're in each other all along."

Jenny says to love Peter is just like breathing. She appreciates that Peter learned English when he spent time in England. She admires his dedication. Without that characteristic and without Jenny's courage they certainly would not be standing here today.

Peter and Jenny are an unconventional "global" couple, very independent and confident, able to pursue such a challenging relationship.

Today, we celebrate two outstanding people who, despite the challenges, obstacles, and extraordinary circumstances, are wonderfully suited to each other. They are committed to create a successful marriage. They are willing to compromise and endure with patience the slow growth and ripening of a good relationship.

ADDENDUM III

Rachov

The town of my birth had many names and was, over the years, incorporated into the governments of many different countries. Back in 1830, it had a total population of 2,446 people with no Jewish residents. By 1921, Rachov had a population of 6,879, including 912 Jews. By 1941, the town had grown to 12,455, 1,707 of whom were Jewish. At that time, many Jews, who were Zionist earlier in the twentieth century, had received pioneer training and had emigrated to Palestine.

In Rachov, as in many towns and cities in Eastern Europe, Jews dominated commercial life. They were craftsmen, factory owners, and shopkeepers. They owned thirty grocery or variety stores, ten textile and ready-made clothing stores and three wholesale food markets.

The Jewish intelligentsia (people with academic credentials) included one judge in the magistrate's court, two doctors, three lawyers and four dentists. They were involved in public life—serving on the municipal council, on governmental committees and holding down government jobs. My family owned the only two bakeries and were involved in town politics.

After the Vienna Agreement of November 2, 1938, the Carpatho-Rus area was annexed to Hungary and the Austro-Hungarian Empire, the Hungarian state of Marmaros, was split. The northern and central areas (everything north of the Tisza River) was turned over to the newly formed state of Czechoslovakia, whereas the southeastern area (south of the Tisza) became part of Romania. Because the town was located in the northern part of Czechoslovakia, it was renamed Rachiv.

Following the Hungarian occupation in March, 1939, some young Jews from Rachiv succeeded in fleeing to the Soviet Union, being among the first to join the Czechoslovakian brigade that fought against the Nazis on the eastern front in 1941. That year the Hungarians drafted many young people into the slave labor battalions, sending them east for forced labor or to the eastern front where many died. That is when my father and other Jewish businessmen from the town fled to Budapest. Also that summer dozens of Jewish families, without proper Hungarian citizenship, were expelled to Kamianets-Podilskyi, a mass extermination camp, where they were killed.

The remaining 950 Jews of Rachiv were deported to Auschwitz in the spring of 1944 where most of them were exterminated. In all, 1,220 Jews from my town perished in the Holocaust, including my grandmother, brother and many other family members. Only a smattering of Jews returned to Rachiv after their liberation. Most left for Israel in the 1970s.

Today Rachiv is a Rain Center (district) in the Zakarpats'ka oblast of Ukraine with a city population of 15,241 inhabitants which includes 83.8% Ukrainians, 11.6% Hungarians, 3.2% Romanians and 0.8% Russians, according to the 2001 census. A few elderly Jewish widows and one Jewish family live there today.

A panorama of Rakhiv.

Rahó, Magyarország

The Rachiv district is home to Ukraine's greatest mountain peaks; it the highest point of Ukraine at an elevation of 430 meters above sea level.

Interesting sights to see in and around Rachiv include the Carpathian Biosphere Reserve, the Museum of Forest Ecology, the highest mountainous waterfall, Truants, and the Geographical Center of Europe marker, located in nearby Dilove (as calculated by the Austro-Hungarian geographers in 1887).

SOURCES

Encyclopedia of Ukraine, Rachov portion of Sefer Mamaros

The Encyclopedia of Jewish Life Before and During the Holocaust (2001)

Wikipedia

(Compiled by Marshall J. Katz with assistance from M.Y. Ehrenreich)

ADDENDUM IV

Glossary of Therapy Terms

The Alexander Technique

"The Alexander Technique is a way of learning how you can get rid of harmful tension in your body. It is a way of learning to move mindfully through life. The Alexander process shines a light on inefficient habits of movement and patterns of accumulated tension, which interferes with our innate ability to move easily and according to how we are designed. It's a simple yet powerful approach that offers the opportunity to take charge of one's own learning and healing process, because it's not a series of passive treatments but an active exploration that changes the way one thinks and responds in activity. It produces a skill set that can be applied in every situation.

Lessons leave one feeling lighter, freer, and more grounded. The Alexander Technique is a method that works to change (movement) habits in our everyday activities. It is a simple and practical method for improving ease and freedom of movement, balance, support and coordination. The technique teaches the use of the appropriate amount of effort for a particular activity, giving you more energy for all your activities. It is not a series of treatments or exercises, but rather a reeducation of the mind and body. The Alexander Technique is a method which helps a person discover a new

balance in the body by releasing unnecessary tension. It can be applied to sitting, lying down, standing, walking, lifting, and other daily activities..."
www.alexandertechnique.com

EST

"Erhard Seminars Training created by Werner Erhard in 1971...EST is also Latin for 'It is.' Its purpose is to offer intensive communications and self-development workshops. The Point of the workshops have transformation in one's natural self-expression rather than living by an inherited set of rules." Wikipedia

Jungian Analysis

"Jungian analysis, which takes place in a dialectical relationship between analyst and analysand, has for its goal the analysand's movement toward psychological wholeness. This transformation of the personality requires coming to terms with the unconscious, its specific structures and their dynamic relations to consciousness as these become available during the course of analysis. Transformation also depends upon the significant modification of the unconscious structures that shape and control ego-consciousness at the beginning of analysis, a change that takes place through the constellation of archetypal structures and dynamics in the interactive field between analyst and analysand."– Murray Stein (1995, p. 33) www.jungian.ca

Reiki

"Reiki (pronounced Ray Key) is a combination of two Japanese words rei and ki meaning universal life energy. Reiki is an ancient laying-on of hands healing technique that uses the life force energy to heal, balancing the subtle energies within our bodies. Reiki addresses physical, emotional, mental and spiritual imbalances. This healing art is an effective delivery system. The Reiki practitioner serves as a vessel that supplies healing energies where they are most needed by the recipient. Reiki's ki-energies flow out of the practitioner's body through the palms of the hands while they are touching the recipient's body." By Phylamana Lila Desy, www.healing.about.com

Rolfing

"Rolfing is a physically applied process, administered by a qualified practitioner, typically in a series of ten sessions with the objective of maximizing individual well-being of body and mind." www.rolfing.org

Rubenfeld Synergy Method

"The Rubenfeld Synergy Method® (RSM®), created by Ilana Rubenfeld, is an alternative healing method which combines touch and talk to help you deal with the stresses in your life. Your symptoms of stress can show up in various ways in your body. Some of the most common symptoms that you may be familiar with are the proverbial "pain in the neck," shouldering "the weight of the world" or feeling overwhelmed, exhausted and "running on empty." Maybe you feel just shut down and have completely lost touch with your body. Rubenfeld Synergy uses your body as the starting point, because your body is home to your thoughts, feelings and your spirit. By exploring these relationships, you can claim a greater role in your own wellness." www. rubenfeldsynergy.com

Tai Chi Chuan

Tai Chi Chuan involves performing slow, graceful exercises that combine movement, meditation, and rhythmic breathing. According to the principles of traditional Chinese medicine, these exercises can help stimulate the flow of vital energy (also known as "chi") and, in turn, promote healing from a variety of heal

"Tai Chi Chuan is a mind-body practice often used to enhance mental and physical health. Although it was initially developed as a martial art, it's commonly practiced as a form of moving meditation. Many practitioners of Tai Chi Chuan use this technique to reduce stress, as well as to improve posture, balance, flexibility, and strength. In addition, Tai Chi Chuan is said to boost mood, alleviate pain, strengthen the immune system, and improve heart health." By Cathy Wong, ND. www.altmedicine.about.com

About the Author

Renée Feller was born in a small Czechoslovakian town. Her mother died when she was six. Her father remarried, so her cousin became her stepmother. Hitler's regime entered the area, and life became precarious, leading to her incarceration at Auschwitz at age thirteen. After the war, she was sent to America, where her new life included three husbands, three daughters (one of whom has Down syndrome), and an ongoing search to recover her feelings and joy in life. She has been in ongoing Jungian analysis, became a Rubenfeld synergist, and at age seventy, was ordained as a rabbi. Now in her ninth decade, she takes Tai Chi Chuan classes and performs interfaith marriages around the world.

Printed in the United States
By Bookmasters